Practical Pre-School Books

Planning for Effective Early Learning

Professional skills in developing a child-centred approach to planning

by Jennie Lindon

Contents

Published by Practical Pre-School Books, A Division of MA Education Ltd, St Jude's Church, Dulwich Road, Herne Hill, London, SE24 0PB.

Tel: 020 7738 5454

www.practicalpreschoolbooks.com

© MA Education Ltd 2011

All photos © MA Education Ltd. Photos taken by Ben Suri.

Front cover (clockwise): © MA Education Ltd 2010, © MA Education Ltd 2011, © MA Education Ltd 2011

ISBN 978-1-907241-15-4

Early Childhood Essentials

Planning that matters for children

Across the UK, national frameworks for early years provision expect that practitioners should use their adult ability to be thoughtful, along with their greater knowledge than any young child can have accumulated. In all the different types of early years provision, adults' effort over planning should enable a breadth of experiences that young children judge to be worth their time and energy: worth exploring, worth talking and thinking about, worth revisiting, recalling and sharing with other people.

Planning matters; I will stand up for the importance of planning as an integral part of best early years practice. Yet a proportion of early years practitioners are uncertain, sometimes anxious, about how to plan in ways that genuinely support children's learning and contribute to an enjoyable and satisfying early childhood.

Planning should enable a breadth of experiences

A very great deal rests upon what early years practitioners believe – and have been told - is meant by the words 'planning' and 'plans'. When practitioners say, "We're supposed to plan", what kind of activity is uppermost in their mind?

In my training and consultancy, I became increasingly aware that, for some of the early years workforce 'planning' exclusively means written plans. There is nothing the matter with writing down forward plans that have evolved from a thoughtful process of planning. When children are involved in planning that is meaningful to them, they are often keen that somebody should, "Write down our important ideas" and "We mustn't forget what we've decided". The problems arise when plans have been drafted in detail, sometimes well in advance and practitioners are uneasy about letting a plan change in response to children's expressed interests on the day. Such problems multiply when the written plan has been created by adults who have no personal knowledge of these individual young children.

This book explores ways to understand the process of looking ahead on behalf of young learners – without getting bogged down in the kind of pre-packaged activity approach that takes the zest out of potentially enjoyable experiences. The book is broken down into three key sections:

- Why is planning important and what is meant by 'planning' and 'plans'? What kind of planning works best to support young children as they learn? (pages 3-14)

- Planning within early childhood provision that flows through the learning environment - with examples to show what best practice for young children looks like in action. (pages 23-35)

- The role of leading good practice: helping others to understand the key issues and pathways to improving current practice. (pages 41-68)

Planning as a flexible and thoughtful process

Why should early years practitioners plan?

Planning does matter; a developmentally appropriate approach to planning can make a positive difference to the experiences of young children. However, the reflective approach that needs to go hand-in-hand with planning starts with this question: "Why plan?". Asking "Why?", or "What for?" if you prefer, addresses the best list of priorities when planning for young children's learning.

The top priority should be that early years practitioners give time and energy to planning in order to benefit the children. You consider what you offer and in what ways, because you are committed to providing experiences that are developmentally appropriate for babies, toddlers and young children. You give energy to getting to know individual children so that anything you plan will be well suited to their age, ability and current interests and preferences. You avoid any kind of planning that rests upon a one-size-fits-all philosophy.

Close behind the benefits to children as an answer to "Why?" should be a focus on the adults who spend their days with young children. Close attention to planning will enable you and your colleagues to keep your knowledge of child development fresh. A sensible approach to planning will allow you to revisit your expectations of what children might be able to do, as well as what are realistic next steps. As a professional the planning process is a good way of keeping you aware of all aspects of development and ensuring that some potential areas of learning do not push aside others.

The answer to "Why should we plan?" should never be "To keep the inspector happy" nor "Because we have to". You do not plan an activity exclusively, or mainly, to meet the goal of showing another adult that you have plans. This answer to the "Why?" question, and the anxiety that usually underpins it, is a warning that practitioners have been persuaded into believing that planning is not a thoughtful process. Instead, planning is

What does useful planning look like?

What might happen if early years practitioners did not bother to plan ahead in any way at all? Children's experiences with you over early childhood could be very limited. However much young boys and girls would love to cook, their familiar adults would never have got around to organising the ingredients, or even better, going out together on a shopping trip.

A great deal depends on what practitioners mean by the word 'planning'. Planning to be able to cook will not be enjoyable if, in practice, this means children are waiting while the adult does almost everything. Then they are allowed to decorate the finished product – and every child will make a fairy cake whether they want to or not.

There is plenty of space for discussion between the two extremes for planning. Young children do not enjoy, nor benefit from, a highly regimented day or session. On the other hand, they are not well supported by practitioners who pass by good opportunities out of fear of 'interfering' with children's play.

in practice no more than written plans – pieces of paper, which may have no benefit for young children at all.

What should the word 'planning' mean?

Planning is an active process, either working as an individual, thoughtful practitioner, or when a small group of people get

Example: planning for young children

Enjoyment with 'in', 'through' and 'out again'

In Grove House Infant and Toddler Centre several children were keen to practise their balancing on a low course created by hard plastic planks resting on blocks and making a five-sided shape. Older toddlers and twos walked around this challenge, with a helping hand available if they wanted it. Several two-year-olds were also enthusiastic about practising their already impressive jumping skills (see page 16).

In terms of planning to support 'next steps', this example is about the literal next steps for very young children. The adult short-term decision was closely linked with what they had observed. A number of the children wanted to balance and an appropriate next step was to offer exactly that opportunity. This option was possible because of the approach to long-term and short-term planning within the Infant and Toddler Centre (ITC) team.

The ITC team had planned ahead over the last year to reorganise their outdoor learning environment. The resources for balancing were a useful reminder, along with the barrel and base, that opportunities for clambering, jumping or balancing do not depend on fixed climbing equipment. In fact, as part of the re-thinking of the under threes outdoor space, the ITC

team had decided to remove a climbing and sliding large piece of equipment, since it occupied quite a lot of space. Their decision had enabled them to bring in separate items of equipment that could be used in a more flexible way to support young children's physical skills. So, within the week of my visit the team had the space to lay out equipment well suited to meet the children's wish to balance, clamber and jump.

The ITC team plan enhancements to the permanent play provision – indoors as well as outside – from what they observe has interested these very young children. These short-term planned changes happen within the week, often the next day and sometimes as an immediate response to something a child does or says (see page 21).

The ITC team, along with the nursery team of Grove House Children's Centre, also apply the skills of planning to ensuring plenty of time for children to become immersed in their current interest. Planning around deployment of adults ensures that practitioners are easily available for children. The shared understanding is that any adult-initiated activity is left flexible for children to influence.

together. You are busy with thinking, talking about, devising and designing what may be done and how, never forgetting the important "Why?" and "So what?"

- The essence of any kind of planning is that you are looking ahead, not always a long time ahead, to create bridges of experience and knowledge between the past, the present and the future.

- Planning that works to the benefit of young children involves a process of bringing your knowledge of individual children, and this age group in general, to bear on the breadth of experiences that will be available to them.

- Planning applies to all aspects of what will make a positive difference to children's daily experiences, including the learning environment and play resources. Active planning also has an impact on timing, routines and the vital backdrop in early childhood provision of nurture.

- Planning also applies to the crucial human resource – the practitioners. Overall organisation needs to ensure that practitioners are available as play companions for babies and young children.

Plans are the result of the process of planning: what emerges from the talking and thinking.

- Sometimes a plan will be a verbal promise or commitment that "Tomorrow we will..." or "Katie will find out about…" Good, even very important, plans are not always written down. Sometimes you, and the children, hold the short-term plan in your mind.

POINT FOR REFLECTION

Choices for planning

Each of the settings described in this book had a different approach to planning in terms of how they were organised for discussion within the team and what kind of supporting paperwork they had developed. However, they shared common ground over the commitment to their ethos of planning as a process, rather than a checklist of activities.

Each team, fully supported by the manager and senior practitioners, placed their knowledge and observation of individual children at the centre of daily and weekly decisions about "What next?" They considered what would be appropriate next steps from the expressed interest of individual children or small groups. There was always a close connection with how a child wanted to use favourite resources or skills they looked keen to practise.

Each team was able to explain what they did, and why – and these descriptions linked closely with the enthusiasm of individual children who attended this provision. These settings shared the commitment to planning but they did not use the same planning or recording paper layouts.

LINKS WITH YOUR PRACTICE

Within my training or consultancy over the last ten years or so, I have spoken with experienced, yet anxious, childminders who were flummoxed. The view could be summed up as, "What do I show the inspector? I work in my own home, not a nursery. I can't do planning." Equally experienced practitioners in group settings, showing very good practice with under threes, would tell me, "We work with babies and toddlers; we can't plan."

These practitioners were thoughtful about what worked for individual children they knew very well. They looked ahead, organised valuable experiences and were always thinking about suitable resources. They had good skills of planning which they applied appropriately. Their professional experience told them that their working situation, and/or the age of the children, would in no way fit written activity plans, with pre-determined learning outcomes.

My role was partly that of agreeing with the professional judgement of these practitioners. But equally I stressed that, in my view they were planning and they operated with suitably open-ended plans. It would have been poor professional practice for them to write very detailed and inflexible intentions for what would happen each day. The remaining issue to discuss was how could they best show and share their good practice – to the inspector, but just as important to share with parents and colleagues in a group setting.

Do these comments relate to your own practice? Are you, or some of your colleagues in your team, still working through this kind of uncertainty?

- Sometimes, a plan is committed to paper and often this capturing of forward thinking uses written words. But often, it is just as useful to have images, simple diagrams or other ways of illustrating "What we are going to do".

- Innovative ways of planning with young children are often documented in visual as well as written plans, sometimes created jointly with the children (see page 25).

Whatever ways you capture your plans on paper – or other stationery – the format should not become more important than the content it contains. Some practitioners find it useful to gather ideas on a spider diagram, or other layouts. Some settings have a simple pro forma. If it works, then keep using your favoured method. There is no single required template – in any of the UK early years frameworks. Some guidance materials, for instance in the CD provided with the English Early Years Foundation Stage (EYFS, 2008) offer examples of possible written formats, with glimpses of the process of planning to support responsible completion of the visual template. But none of these possible models are statutory (required); they are all within the context of suggestions, and should be read as guidance rather than compulsory formats that you must follow.

Best practice over early childhood across the UK has never been a watered down version of the current primary school curriculum. Early childhood is a qualitatively different developmental phase from that of primary education and the classroom model does not fit young children's intellectual or emotional needs, nor does a lesson plan approach. This inflexible view of lesson planning creaks badly when applied to the learning of older fours and fives. The approach starts to fragment when applied to young fours and threes, and shatters if practitioners are directed to organise babies, toddlers and twos with pre-determined adult-led events. Under threes are very interested in a wide range of play and conversation, some of which is introduced by a familiar adult. However, they are not developmentally ready to cope with adult-led group activities, with all the waiting and turn taking which that requires.

The birth to five childhood range of the EYFS in England highlighted that sound knowledge of child development has to move practitioners away from a very directive view of planning as looking the same across all of early childhood. Good early years practice with the under threes is highlighted in different ways in other parts of the UK, in particular the Pre-Birth to Three guidance in Scotland (Learning and Teaching Scotland, 2010). At the other end of the age range, good primary school practice

Longer term planning ensures the time to be with children

must rest on acknowledgement of how younger children learn and that children do not suddenly become 'pupils' once they walk through the school gates. It is important to note that reception class (in England) is the final year of the Early Years Foundation Stage, not the first year of statutory schooling.

Long term planning

It makes sense to view planning as a process that operates within different time scales, depending on the nature of what you are considering. The teams in all the settings mentioned in this book planned over timescales that included long term through to very short term.

Good early years practice is to look ahead, as well as to focus on today. The long-term perspective can stretch up to a year and may include:

- Developments that need careful reflection within the senior team. For instance, the Kennet Day Nursery senior team had made significant changes in recent years. They had supported internal change step-by-step by developing effective ways for practitioners to be highly responsive to child-initiated learning. As this approach became more fully understood in the team and confidence grew, they decided

LINKS WITH YOUR PRACTICE

Teams and individual childminders use long-term planning to reflect in a broad way about what they hope young children will be enabled to learn and how the adults currently offer experiences.

There should be a strong focus on how the adults behave, or think they should behave towards young children. For instance, you might look closely at the pattern of communication in your provision, maybe because you are concerned that many of the children have limited skills of listening and talking.

Possible questions for reflection could be:

- Are adults communicative with young children?

- Is there plenty of time in the normal day for sustained conversations rather than adult-directed question-and-answer?

- Are there comfortable spaces where it feels right to relax and chat – for children who are friends as well as between adults and children?

POINT FOR REFLECTION

Learning within unplanned events

The example on page 9 from Garfield reception class demonstrates how much can be happening within an absorbing sequence that was not planned as an activity by practitioners. Yet planning was involved. This lengthy exploration of the roof of the shed was possible because the Garfield team have planned a day in which there is generous time for such an event to unfold. The team have also addressed practical issues around a learning environment which is safe enough for children to choose to take manageable risks.

The events around the shed had not been planned in advance, with associated learning outcomes. Yet there is good reason to say that these children were showing evidence of past learning and, for a practitioner who knew them, possible new developments.

In an English reception class it is appropriate to consider children's learning in terms of the early learning goals. Look at your copy of the EYFS Statutory Guidance (2008, pages 12-16) and consider which ELGs it is fair to say are reflected in this example. I will start your thoughts with the ELG in Personal, Social and Emotional Development about working as part of a group and taking turns. Also the goal in Communication, Language and Literacy about interacting with others and negotiating plans. Choose your own ELG(s) from Physical Development.

there was no longer any need to plan through topics with the over threes. See also the significant change of direction taken by Sun Hill Infant School described on page 43.

- Sometimes you need to gather information and ideas about possibilities – whether for a change in practice or reorganising your indoor or outdoor environment, with the input from children. Sometimes the forward planning will involve identifying sources of funding.

- Continued professional development for team members or individual childminders needs a longer term view that considers what is the gap in the adults' experience, or what needs refreshing in terms of skills.

- Effective teams and individual childminders take the longer term view in order to ensure that they value all the areas of development and understand fully how different areas of learning work together for young children. For instance,

some teams have made efforts to ensure that they do not underestimate the importance of physical development and the value of being physically active (page 15).

Long term planning can never be about the details of what individual children will do in the future. So concern about children's communication skills should not simply trigger a list of extra activities or purchase of resources, without thorough discussion about what has really been missing from the children's experience to date. Positive long-term planning looks at the learning potential of play experiences and important routines for children. Reflection and discussion needs to ensure that you are very aware of the potential learning from particular resources, experiences and significant times of the day.

Example: child-initiated learning

Very young children need the personal touch

Look at the two descriptions that follow and think about:

● In a broad sense, what kind of planning has happened in these early years settings to enable the personal approach shown in each example? You could look back at the bullet points on page 8 for some hints.

● The practitioners did not plan for these events to happen; they responded to the interests of the babies or children on this day. But a lot of thoughtfulness sits behind what I was able to observe on my visit.

1. Going with the flow for babies

The Oakfield Nursery Baby Unit occupies two large rooms with separate changing and sleeping areas. The focus on planning for this very young group has been through a welcoming, comfortable physical environment, easy availability of the adults and routines that follow the needs of individual babies and toddlers. The atmosphere was relaxed and calm and I watched as practitioners interacted with babies and toddlers in a very personal way. This approach is possible because the team is thoughtful about use of space.

● One practitioner sat with two young toddlers in a comfortable corner where the children could access books of their own choosing. With one toddler on her lap and another close by, she enjoyed a series of books with the one toddler, whilst being available to the second toddler, who was happy to look at his own book.

● Other practitioners were on the floor with babies and toddlers, following the choices of those children from a range of floor toys. There was a relaxed feel to the rooms and toddlers were able to move about easily. The adults remained relatively still.

● Four toddlers had chosen to get involved in tabletop printing. They wielded their choice of sponge, cotton reel and other means of printing and painting. The practitioner at this low table remained sitting with the children, helped if they indicated they wanted assistance and took some photos of the experience.

● Some background music played at one point during the morning and one toddler was resting against a low table. She started to move her body in time with music, still holding on

Example: child-initiated learning

securely to the table. Her dancing was immediately noticed and welcomed. The toddler looked pleased with the positive attention and reactions from the adults.

Another practitioner sat on part of the long sofa, which stretches along one wall. She was bottle feeding one baby, taking her time and talking gently to Michael (7 months old). When Michael was completely finished, the practitioner sat on the floor with him and shared toys one at a time, giving him plenty of scope to explore the toy in whatever way he wished. She used a puppet to tickle his tummy and touched him gently. Michael reacted with a stream of giggles and so the practitioner repeated this game several times. Then she offered some simple sound solid shapes and Michael explored each in turn, as the practitioner demonstrated how to shake the item and that different ones made different sounds. Michael showed a renewed interest in the puppet, so the practitioner picked up the puppet once more and that game continued.

The Baby Unit indoor space opens onto a small area which leads by steps up into the main garden. The doors were open to the lower outdoor section, with foam mats creating a soft surface. Babies and toddlers were therefore able to move into and explore this contained small outdoor area and be seen clearly from inside the nearest indoor space. A gate meant that they could not leave this area and climb the steps out of sight. Later in the day the practitioners went out into the garden with babies and toddlers.

2. Child-initiated learning in reception class

The Garfield reception class team focus on planning through a very well resourced indoor and outdoor environment which children access in free flow for most of the day. The focussed planning for each week leads through a small number of focus children and their chosen focus of exploration. Other boys and girls usually opt to join in this child-led, adult-supported project. Daily planning and reflection with the children happens within group times at the beginning and end of the morning and the afternoon (Lindon, 2010d).

I was able to observe boys and girls fully engaged in a range of self-chosen pursuits. The children were active intellectually as well as physically. The planning over use of time, and practitioners as the vital human resource, meant that the adults were all easily available as a play and conversational partner with children throughout the day.

Four boys were busy building with blocks and they were well able to build and talk at the same time. They engaged the adult in a conversation about which children were present today and who was away. The practitioner went through the names with them and then followed the boys' lead in a play-related conversation that ranged widely. The boys wanted to talk about what was being built, the significance of the animal figures used within the construction and the fact that some seemed to be broken. The discussion moved on to what could be done about mending them. Then they heard music and wondered why it sounded familiar. They agreed it sounded like the Star Wars theme.

Like other places I visited for this book, the Garfield team has taken care to leave scope for adventure in their outdoor environment. It is noticeable that, given these opportunities, the girls are also physically active and manage their own risk for clambering and jumping. During the morning, some children became interested in what was on the roof of the outdoor shed. This permanent storage is at the entrance to a 'wild' area which contains tyres, barrels and low trees which children can climb. First one adult, and then a second team member, was close by as the children worked out how to see on top of the shed. They created a workable system of steps and a large block. One child at a time clambered up and had a good look up onto the roof. Children were very patient as they waited for their turn.

Conversation flowed in the group and I listened to the second adult as he recalled with the children their previous enterprises in this area of the garden. The children showed pleasure in talking about what they had done in the past. The conversation turned to the current focus of being high enough to be able to look onto the actual shed roof. One child wondered why they should not clamber onto the roof itself. The practitioner explained, "The roof isn't strong enough". The child then questioned, "But I'm strong enough". The practitioner went on, "I'm sure you're strong enough. The roof isn't strong enough to have children on it".

At this point one boy rolled across a large barrel with the suggestion that it would be easier to climb up with this addition – which proved to be a good idea. The practitioner let children know that it would soon be time to tidy up. He managed the last turn and anticipated through conversation who would take which job in getting the equipment of the clambering system back to its storage place.

LINKS WITH YOUR PRACTICE

The team from Kate Greenaway Nursery School and Children's Centre (2009) considered what they called Core Experiences. They identified a range of experiences which were available to children every day, or on a very regular basis and which were suitable across the full age range, with minor adjustments. This team homed in on fourteen experiences, which included sand and water play, block play, cooking, trips out to the neighbourhood and gardening.

Through discussion the centre team acknowledged that opportunities for a valuable experience like gardening could be too intermittent, perhaps triggered by the arrival of spring. They decided to offer gardening to the children all year round. This change in longer term planning led to realising how much children learn by repeated involvement around a central experience.

The adults became very aware that growing and tending plants is a different enterprise when undertaken in wintertime, compared with the summer. Children's sustained involvement in all aspects of gardening and, where appropriate cooking what they had grown, highlighted how every aspect of development was supported by this meaningful experience.

For instance, a well-resourced block play corner will support physical skills and meaningful, direct experience of early mathematical concepts. But young children who have plenty of relaxed time to construct with blocks also communicate with each other, and adult play companions. They chat, they plan joint enterprises and they often use the blocks, with other imported materials, to support their pretend play (Community Playthings, 2005.) So long as children are in a learning environment where it is perfectly understood that can move materials to where they are needed, sustained block play may also bring in skills on the journey towards literacy. Young children sometimes want to have notices as part of some constructions. They may want to draw a design that is especially successful. Taking a photo is a useful option, but many children still enjoy making paper copies.

Young children have the potential to learn in every aspect of their development, when they have the time and space to use a valuable play resource such as good quality blocks. Forward planning includes practitioner awareness of, for instance, how access to the block corner can support creative development across the age range of early childhood. If you spend your day with older fours and fives then it makes sense to be aware of the early learning goal that includes exploring shape and space in two and three dimensions. However, if you work with younger children, then you need to be looking for the three-year-old version or the toddler version of enjoying construction

A resource like water can be available in different ways

Children concentrate on their chosen focus

Example: looking ahead to support learning

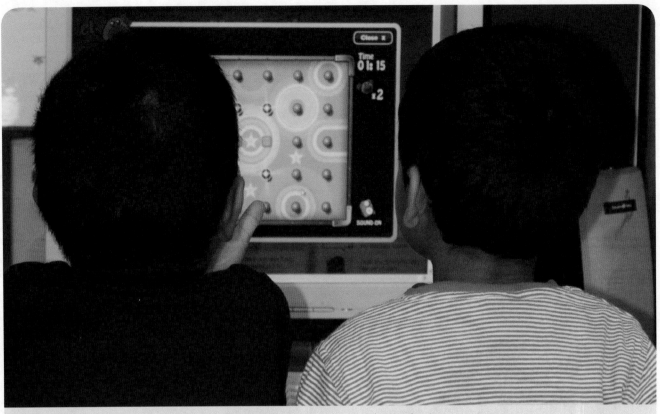

Can children choose to work together?

The children in Sun Hill reception class had generous time to follow their own chosen pursuits (page 19). The observation-led planning meant that adult-initiated activities and any enhancements to the environment were based on practitioners' high alertness to what currently interested children and ways in which they were keen to learn more.

A flexible termly plan listed some highlights from the broad areas of learning in the EYFS.

- The focus of 'What do we want the children to learn' was selected on the firm basis of knowing children very well, and what they already understood. The forward planner had suggestions of the kind of vocabulary that it would be sensible to introduce over this time period.

- Another section of the forward planning listed a range of adult-initiated experiences which answered 'How will we enable this learning to take place?'

- This forward plan for the adult contribution to the term's experiences also rested on continued alertness within the team to what children were learning effectively from their self-chosen experiences.

- The team remained open-minded about the likely pattern of learning and there was no expectation that a given activity would definitely ensure one aspect of learning in particular.

- A final section of the forward planner asked, 'How will we know who has learned what?'. There were some possibilities to look out for and, since the children were in an English reception class, these items were taken from the EYFS Profile.

The Sun Hill reception team, completely supported by their Head, decided they had to take a responsible professional stance over unrealistic literacy early learning goals in the EYFS. Specific reading and handwriting goals have been challenged by a significant number of early years specialists, for instance Palmer and Bayley (2004) and Moyles (2006). The Sun Hill team explain the usual pattern of child development to parents and show that help is available if children are genuinely struggling on the basis of realistic expectations. By the end of Key Stage One children are literate and that is the more realistic expectation.

Example: planning for the full possibilities of learning

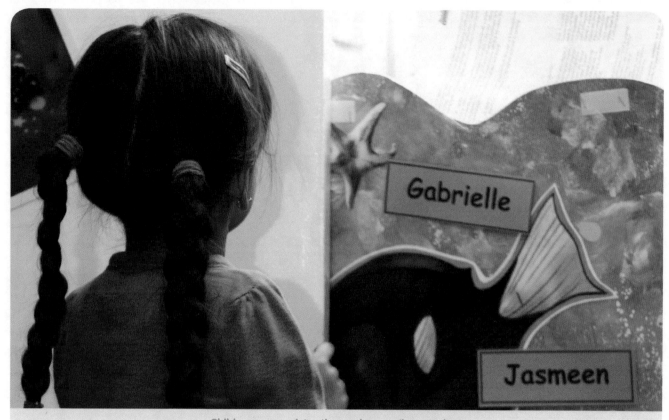

Children can register themselves as 'here today'

There is a notice board in the main entrance hall of Oakfield Nursery School and everyone involved in the nursery has their photo on this board: the senior team, practitioners who work directly with the children, the cook, administrative and domestic team members, and people who provide special experiences on particular days such as dance and football. The message is that everyone is important and contributes to the experiences of young children at the setting.

The Oakfield team regard planning as an active process and focus a great deal on keeping alert to the full learning potential of experiences, different indoor and outdoor areas, resources and routines. The aim is to sharpen up everyone's awareness of what children could gain and to avoid any limited views that this activity or resource will definitely lead to this kind of learning. Over time the team has built up extensive documentation from their reflection and discussion and materials reflect all areas of learning and development from the EYFS.

A4 laminated sheets have been created for many aspects of the continuous provision, such as access to sand or water, and also for important routines within the normal day. These visual reminders weave in possible learning opportunities for babies and children from all aspects of their development. The focus is on the potential for children, for instance the range of opportunities from small world resources, music or mark making.

The laminated sheets are a refresher and support for the team but also a way of communicating with parents. For instance, in the Baby Unit there is a clear visual message that the nappy changing routine is important for babies and is regarded as valuable time by the key person of that baby or toddler. At the other end of the age range, the eldest children are involved in self-registration. Reasons for choosing an active, rather than passive routine, are shown in a display of what children learn by finding their name and registering themselves.

Large folders have been created as team projects to keep fresh on the possibilities. Some binders include photos of particular resources with descriptions of the likely learning opportunities for children. Some completed binders have been created with one or two practitioners taking the main responsibility to look at issues like ICT throughout the nursery, or making the very most of the outdoor environment.

materials. One option is to look at the Development Matters column on pages 110-2 in the EYFS Guidance (DCSF, 2008).

In practice, the different perspectives on planning are related to each other and not completely separate adult activities. Longer term planning should be linked with what you have observed of the children and what you have learned from what they showed or told you.

Adult thoughtfulness in all provision should be applied to observation-led plans for how to enhance the learning environment, or to organise special experiences that take more time, funding or creative resourcing. These longer term plans eventually become shared with children. They should be offered an active part in short term decision-making about what to do with the weedy bit of the garden or how we get the policeman and his horse to come back and visit us again. So long as you have made changes to get a vital resource like water available in your outdoors area, then children will show you what they want to do with this resource today.

A medium term planning perspective tends to be no longer than a couple of months and that timescale tends to operate when settings run a flexible topic-based approach for the over-threes (see page 66). This kind of forward planning always has plenty of scope for short-term changes. It is not appropriate in early years to have rolling programmes of topics, projects or activities

Basic resources work best

The construction of wall displays in Oakfield Nursery School gives a clear visual message that children are active in determining the flow of experiences. Photos always show the process of an activity or event and so communicate the message that a successful activity is not exclusively about end products.

A display in the Baby Unit showed how older babies and toddlers had recently been exploring the piles of leaves fallen from the trees into the garden. Parents could see that their children had been given plenty of time to get right into the leaves. Some toddlers had also got stuck into painting simple leaf shapes and this experience was also part of the display.

The thoughtfulness of the team about learning opportunities is also reflected in communication with families through some wall displays. The displays are also of direct interest to the children. For instance in the Toddlers and Tweenies (18 months to nearly three years), there are six sets of photos that illustrate, 'What happens in…' and the areas covered are the changing room, the dining room, our imaginative room, outdoor play, our creative room and our physical room. The photos capture visually what children do and then two other boxes describe in words, 'Some of the things we might do' and 'Some of the things we might learn'.

A slightly different layout for the two rooms for the over threes communicates the same messages with photos of how children spend their days and what they are enabled to learn over time from different experiences and their active involvement in routines.

- In what ways do you show, as well as tell, parents about how you think about the experiences you offer to the children?

- If any parents seem to judge success by something to take home, have you unintentionally encouraged this view?

- Think about what you showcase by wall displays and be ready to encourage and help children to share what they did, rather than sound apologetic that nothing has been made.

Think about timing for group experiences

Relaxed time for routines like tidying

LINKS WITH YOUR PRACTICE

Young children benefit from your thoughtfulness about planning resources. But sometimes adults can get too complicated for children's own good. It usually works best to have a generous supply of simple resources and leave children to determine the level of complexity for how the resource is used.

● Have plenty of good quality wooden blocks rather than a range of small-scale construction kits, which are unlikely to have sufficient parts for serious building by several children at a time.

● Collect real telephones or mobiles (with batteries and SIM cards removed) and let children determine how they are used in pretend play. Avoid battery-operated toy telephones that make random sounds.

● Young children will invent their own sound sequences with simple musical instruments, or pots and pans (see page 6). Children have a voice and will learn to make tuneful trills and sing, when they spend their days with adults who are happy to break into a song or rhyme.

planned months in advance that will be followed no matter which children are present on that day. Early years settings do not all use topic-based planning and, without a topic focus, the medium-term planning tends to be more like two to three weeks. Practitioners then plan ahead on the basis of children's current interests, sometimes around the key group times.

Flexibility in the short term

Some plans may be firm and will be definitely followed, unless unforeseen circumstances disrupt the event. Perhaps you have agreed with the children that together you will make a new batch of playdough tomorrow. Maybe you have committed yourself to collect bags of clean autumn leaves at the weekend and bring them in on Monday morning. Young children should be confident that familiar adults will keep their promises. However, in both instances the children will determine what they choose to do with the new resources.

Some plans involve other people and it would set a bad example of discourtesy to the children if the commitment were cancelled at short notice. Perhaps the local dentist has promised to come and talk with children during their play session linked with the local

Example: long-term planning for opportunities today

Ladybirds Pre-School has a dedicated indoor movement area. The pre-school team created the space following local training about Developmental Movement Play from the national organisation Jabadao (www.jabadao.org/). The leader and her team had also thought a great deal about opportunities for lively and adventurous physical play within their outdoor area (Lindon, 2010d).

The creation of the indoor movement area required the team to think about how they used space. Final decisions had been linked with a change in routine from a sit-down snack time for everyone to developing a rolling snack time. This change has worked very well for the children and also needs less indoor space to be available for a whole group routine.

The indoor developmental movement area is visually clear as a dedicated space that children enter. At the front, four laminated mats with shapes to place shoes remind children that this is a 'shoes off' space and holds a maximum of four children at a time. These simple ground rules enable the children to enjoy vigorous physical play, along with using the foam shapes to build.

Thoughtful, longer term planning lies behind this change in the learning environment: the planned, permanent indoor provision for Ladybirds. But day by day the children decide when and how they access this opportunity. I watched a sustained sequence of busy children in the movement area, accompanied by a practitioner. The adult was led by the children in what she said and did, including the point at which she joined them within the area, because the children had directly invited her.

Jon, Sally and Marsha (threes and fours) were very active in moving the large foam cylinders around to create their own environment in which to leap about, roll, jump and clamber. There was a great deal of chanting along with the clambering: "I'm the king of the castle" and "Ring a ring a roses". It was noticeable in Ladybirds, as in the other early years settings I visited, that young girls are just as physically lively as the boys, when they experience the positive encouragement of space, time, suitable resources and an accepting adult.

Sally was doing a sequence of jumps and called to the practitioner – who was at that point just outside the area - "Count how many jumps I'm doing". The practitioner counted as requested, out loud and used her fingers to show the numbers as she went. This is a good example of using numerical skills for a good reason: that a child wants to count right now. Generally the children most wanted an admiring adult onlooker; there were frequent cries of, "Look, look!" and "Watch me!" The practitioner was then directly invited into the movement area by the children, who wanted her assistance in building. Marsha suggested, "We could make a slide" and the practitioner put back, "How could we make a slide?", inviting their ideas and helping when and where requested.

The children pulled across the foam shapes and a construction developed. Over time they decided it was a house and the practitioner was informed, "You have to knock to come in" and instructed to say, "Knock, knock". The practitioner followed the orders and was part of a sequence of being welcomed into the house, going out and back again.

At one point the practitioner was kneeling and Marsha came very close, choosing to compare her height with that of the adult. A spontaneous conversation evolved, led by Marsha, about how tall she was under these circumstances. Marsha made herself even taller by stepping onto the practitioner's bent knees and comparing once more: now she was taller than the adult. The young girl led the conversation onto when and whether she would ever be really taller than the practitioner. The adult wondered aloud what Marsha would need to do in order to grow taller. Marsha then said she would need lots of good food. She started to list what kinds of food she believed would help her grow.

This exchange was in no sense a planned conversation. That kind of unwise pre-packaging of otherwise spontaneous communication usually disrupts the very skills it allegedly promotes. However, wise adult planning lay behind the opportunity that was seized by this young child. The Ladybirds team are very thoughtful about time, timing and the role of practitioners in close relationships with children. The adults are very available to children; I saw many instances of this kind of genuine conversational exchange within my day at the pre-school.

After about 15 minutes of shared play and conversation, the practitioner left to join another child who was busy playing with the cars. The children, now three girls, continued with active physical play in their special area.

Example: jumping twos

Ready to jump

One aspect to the planning in Grove House Infant and Toddler Centre (ITC) is that the team plan ahead in the light of practitioners' observations of two key children each week. The special activities, that enhance the continuous indoor and outdoor play provision, are chosen to reflect current interests.

A few days before my visit the planned activity for outdoors had been a range of opportunities for jumping. Several children had shown that they were very motivated to practise this physical skill. The team explained to me that many of the toddlers and twos had been active jumping up and down on the ground and in and out of shapes. As usual, the planned activity engaged more young children than the key individuals whose interests led to this planned activity. This opportunity had fine-tuned the skills of several young children, who continued to get ever better at their jumping.

I watched several older toddlers and twos who were enthusiastic about clambering, jumping and balancing. They had a large shape, like a barrel laid on its side, but with a secure base. Two children, a boy and a girl, were especially keen to clamber onto this barrel, steady themselves with care and jump off onto the soft landing area. One or two children were able to convert their jump into a simple roll. Adult help was on offer if they wanted, but one two-year-old boy was particularly stable and needed no help.

I was told that the day before he and the little girl had wanted to get onto this barrel shape. Initially they needed a lot of help but had been practising this move for much of yesterday. They were now adept and had been able to get so competent, because the team ensured that equipment continued to be available to fit their personal interest in becoming really good climbers and jumpers. The children had learned to balance their jump and land by holding their arms out at right angles to their body, pulling in their arms as they landed. The adults close by also had their arms out in the reminder action, as children steadied themselves for the jump. A hurrah went up from the adults, with equal enthusiasm for each and every jump.

Practitioners who work with under threes are sometimes uncertain about how to plan from the interests of very young boys and girls who are unlikely to say in words 'I want to…' This example illustrates that children tell you very clearly by what they choose to do.

childminding network group. Or the local library has organised an extra session with the story teller exclusively for your nursery.

Other plans carry an equal level of commitment, but the details can remain fluid, depending on what seizes children's interests. For instance, you can have a range of practical ideas for following up on the dentist's visit or the storytelling session. But these possible conversations, or exploration through pretend play, evolve in the days that follow and are dependent on how children react to the initial experience. Discussion between colleagues, plus any written forward planning about this kind of event, has to be around possibilities of what children might gain from the experience. Effective planning for young children's experiences becomes derailed if pre-written learning objectives or intentions are treated as inflexible.

Early years practitioners are in a sustained relationship with young children – especially through the key person approach (Lindon, 2010c). You should know them well enough that you can often – not always - make a good guess about what is likely to engage their interest. Your personal knowledge is also crucial for subtle decisions about the level at which an adult-led or organised activity should be pitched. It is fine to have some well-informed hopes for what familiar children will learn from an experience. However, serious problems arise when practitioners hold tight to the learning objectives they wrote into their plan and attempt to direct children's play or conversation to fit those objectives.

POINT FOR REFLECTION

More than one focus for potential learning

In the earlier example, the Infant and Toddlers Centre team of Grove House had judged that it was a good time to focus on several children's strong motivation to enhance their physical skills of large movement. However, within this experience it was equally possible to see how children's self confidence was growing. They made choices about what equipment they wanted to use and when. Some children decided to push the boundaries of what they were able to do and, in two year old version, were managing their own risk in a physically adventurous activity.

At first glance the example highlights physical development but the experience also supported aspects of young children's personal, social and emotional development.

- In what ways do you, or your team, ensure that you lead this week through what you have noticed that children are motivated to explore?

- But, do you also share well-supported judgements about what children have probably also learned, in addition to those skills which could be directly observed?

Using ICT alongside other resources

Plenty of hands-on activity

It does not matter how well you know the children, some aspects of important learning for them will not be obvious until they are fully engaged in an experience. Often it is not clear what children have gained until some time after an event – when what seized their attention emerges through their chosen play or spontaneous conversation with you.

All the early years frameworks across the UK describe several areas of learning, which are relevant for young children. The wording varies, as does the way in which similar developmental areas are organised. But the aim of each framework is that early years practitioners do not overlook any area of development, nor work on the assumption that some aspects of young learning are more important than others. The message is not that plans should be locked onto one area of development. The great excitement of spending your days with young children is that they are delightfully open-minded about what they find absorbing within good quality basic resources or a good adult starter idea. There is no aspect of child development that can only be 'delivered' through a given activity or item of play equipment.

Young children benefit from a flow to their day which means that different types of experiences may happen at different times of the day, or week. Young boys and girls enjoy special activities that fit their skills and interests. However, their learning is not well supported when practitioners believe it is good practice to organise different tables or areas and to move children from one to another according to inflexible adult-determined timing.

The rationale behind this carousel approach, which still exists in some provision, is that over a day or session children will experience every aspect of an early years framework. The argument is also sometimes that, without being moved on by the adults, some children will spend all their time with the same resources or in only one area. This approach rests on a profound misunderstanding of the nature of learning.

● Young children do not only use their emergent counting skills when sat at the table with 'mathematical' resources.

● They certainly do not only extend their language skills in an adult-led 'communication activity'. In fact, adult-directed group time is a far less promising environment than ensuring adults are easily available for spontaneous conversation with young children (Cousins, 2003).

● In a well resourced learning environment, children will use and extend counting or communication skills in many different activities.

● Moving children on to another table or area on a regular basis simply disrupts their concentration. The small group who are keen to spend most of their morning in the construction area, or running their puppet theatre, will definitely extend a wide range of skills. Observant practitioners just need to notice.

Good early years practice is avoiding any sense that distinct areas of learning and development can be 'taught-and-ticked', then onto the next item on the list. The way forward is to use adult planning skills to resource a positive learning environment (more on page 30) and, if necessary, help children who have been previously over-organised by adults, to feel confident to use those resources. Good planning also involves how you manage timing and space(s) in a thoughtful way that enables long runs of uninterrupted time, enabling young children to concentrate on their chosen endeavours.

Sometimes children are enthusiastic about your company but – today at least – have a different idea about what they would like to do, perhaps in your regular key group time together. Only unwise early years practitioners trudge on with an activity that children have clearly let you know has not caught their interest. For instance, perhaps you had good reasons for planning to share books about trucks and other large-scale transport with

Able to spend as much time as they need

Example: time for digging deep holes

Adults show they have time to play

And they value how children want to play

In Sun Hill Reception Class children were busy indoors and in the outdoor area with a wide range of child-initiated enterprises. The children were trusted to move independently within an environment where practitioners were easily available to children throughout the indoors and outdoor areas.

Several boys spent most of one morning digging impressive holes at the far end of the garden. They were keen that their reception teacher should come and see. I also joined them and listened as this enthusiastic group of five-year-olds talked about their chosen project. They explained that they were digging a fox hole. One boy started a conversation about how he was sure he had seen a wolf, but then rethought and said it could well have been a fox. Their teacher was clearly delighted to be given the tour. She listened carefully to their descriptions and the boys' speculation about holes they knew they had not dug.

This busy thinking was brought back to the focussed sit-down time at the end of the morning: the Sun Hill 'Learn-It' times (page 59). The boys were articulate about what they had learned, in this instance about the technical problems in digging up stumps and the requirement for water. The teacher encouraged the boys to explain to the small group why they needed the water. One of the digging crew described in detail how they had dug three big holes and their plans for a fourth. He explained that their goal was to attract animals to the holes, hoping for rabbits, foxes or badgers. The other children in the group became very engaged in how this goal was to be achieved. The teacher made the decision to let this animated discussion run for most of the rest of the group time.

Children other than the diggers started to share ideas about how would anyone know if these animals came and used the holes, because they only came out at night – the word 'nocturnal' was introduced. The teacher encouraged the sharing of ideas with questions such as "How will we know?" and "What might you do?". All the children discussed how it might be possible to get evidence that animals had come to the holes in the night-time. Their main idea was that they would have to be in the garden at night. The teacher set the children what she called 'a challenge': to think about what might be an alternative if families would not let the children stay in the school garden at night. The group time ended with children still thinking about, "How else can we find out, if we can't be here?"

Example: observation-led planning

Music from pots and pans

The senior team in Grove House Children's Centre is organised so that practitioners can plan ahead through discussion in a team meeting. The ITC team works with with three large A3 sheets to plan ahead on a weekly basis for special activities to enhance the continuous indoor and outdoor provision. One sheet applies to the back indoor space (the babies' base room), another to the front space (the toddlers' base room) and the third to their shared under threes outdoor environment. For each day of the upcoming week, there is a special activity planned for morning and afternoon in each of these spaces.

Practitioners contribute their observations of two key children, who have been their special focus over the week. The key person looks in detail at the baby or child's current interests and also considers possible gaps in their development so far, a pattern of progress that is documented by individual learning maps. Possibilities are discussed in the team and written onto the planner for next week.

Additional resources and the small number of adult-led activities to be on offer for the children are chosen on the basis of what has happened this week. The most usual pattern is that activities or experiences planned with one or two children in mind then engage their peers. The large sheets have space not only for 'What goes out/is prepared' but also for the important 'What happened?', a section which is completed day by day and includes brief descriptions of how children reacted to the special opportunities. The observations lead back into an informed discussion of 'What next?'

On the day of my visit one of the special activities was a set of pots, pans and wooden spoons which were used with enthusiasm by a series of children. The resources were laid out in the back room but available to any child. I watched a two-year-old girl very busy with sound making, lining herself up to hit the pots, listening to the sounds, and looking carefully at what to hit next. At times other children and one of the practitioners joined her (see also the photograph on page 6).

The ITC team had good reason to expect that one or two children would be intrigued by musical sound making. But the sustained enthusiasm of several young children – not only the two-year-old whom I watched – let the team know that this special activity could certainly be repeated soon. They were also able to consider in what ways they might supplement the permanent provision of items suitable for vigorous sound making.

Example: seizing the moment

Time to chat as well as ride

Recreating Humpty Dumpty

In Grove House Infant and Toddler Centre many of the very young children were currently keen on Humpty Dumpty and the team were responding to this interest. The children had become very familiar with the book, which was in their current batch from the library. The ITC team told me how several children had spontaneously acted out the story in the garden, as well as requesting many readings of the actual book.

During my visit I watched a series of older toddlers and twos who were as keen as ever to sit on the edge of the low planters, 'fall' off and lay on the ground saying 'broken'. The adults cooperated in 'mending' the Humpties, who continued to insist they were still 'broken'. At one point a practitioner fetched the book from indoors and several children enjoyed hearing the story again. Their preference was to maintain that Humpty could not be mended, despite the fact that in the re-telling for this book he was put together again with glue.

Polar bears join the water feature

In Ladybirds Pre-School several children were involved at different times in creating an impressive water feature.

The enterprise started when Darren organised a stretch of guttering to rest on a milk crate and slope into the tuff spot. He persevered in filling it with water, bucket by bucket, until there was sufficient for his boat to float. Darren then brought three small animal figures to place in the new environment and, joined by two other children, become especially interested in polar bears. The practitioner, who had remained involved, mentioned that there might still be some polar bears in the freezer. (They had been frozen for a previous play exploration.) The practitioner and Darren went off, returning with several polar bears frozen in their own small blocks of ice.

Several children became very interested in this event, explaining, "The polar bears are trapped in the ice". For over 10 minutes several children continued to add water, check the ice around the polar bears and the chunks of free ice that were now floating in the full tuff spot. One child explained clearly to the adult that the ice was melting, getting smaller and smaller. A search started for the smallest – the 'baby polar bears' – until they were discovered in the water.

your key group. But some of the group have looked across from your comfortable seating area in the garden and spotted another key group busy with bats, balls and beanbags.

The wise adult decision with young children is to answer 'yes' to the, "Can we do that?" question. If there are limited resources, your answer might be, "We can definitely do something like that". You focus on the children's chosen activity and later you consider what they probably gained. There is no need to try to rescue some of your original plan by finding a book about playing physical games. Books, trucks and the like have not gone forever; they are just postponed for now.

Time to watch before deciding to join

When to think short, medium or long term

The short-term planning works very well in settings because practitioners think long-term when that is appropriate. Making plans into the future is a sensible use of time, energy and discussion when good ideas about resources and the learning environment will take time to implement. Long-term planning is also important when a senior team is working hard to build the confidence of practitioners to go with the flow of what enthuses young children today. You have

planned for a range of possibilities; sensible early years practitioners do not behave as if they know exactly what is going to happen today. Then you are available and comfortable to go with the flow.

KEY POINTS IN MAKING PLANNING A FLEXIBLE PROCESS

The professional activity of planning should make a positive difference to the daily life of young children in any kind of early years provision.

- Planning should be a process of thinking ahead, which includes specific plans to do something. But 'planning' does not only mean written plans.

- Familiar adults also introduce new experiences they have good reason to expect will enthuse babies and children.

- Planning that benefits babies and under fives also introduces experiences which familiar adults have good reason to predict will enthuse babies and children.

- Planning is not all about activities; it is just as much about time and timing, resources accessible within the learning environment and best use of adults.

- Long-term planning will benefit children through the learning environment and growing skills of the adults.

- Suitable adult-initiated activities for children have to be part of short-term planning, because they need to link with current interests and understanding.

- Practitioners need to become comfortable with the uncertainty of real play and to share control with children over the direction of promising experiences.

- Practitioners need to be alert for busy learning within events that are not planned by adults, but evolve spontaneously from play or conversation.

- Within daily life the opportunities created through long-term planning work together with the moment-by-moment decisions of really short term planning.

Chapter 2

Planning through the learning environment

This book started with questions around the meaning of the word 'planning': what should it mean and what has the term come to mean for some early years practitioners. Significant problems arise when practitioners believe planning begins and ends with written plans for adult-led activities. The current interests of young children become less important than what the adults have decided in advance that everyone will do today. But also the adult skills of planning fail to be applied to the whole learning environment offered to young children.

Enabling environments

Over the last decade or so a considerable amount of rethinking around best practice for young children has focussed on how adults can plan a learning environment that engages children's interest, their enthusiasm and which enables them to make choices for themselves. Adult energy and thoughtfulness – and planfulness – is directed at creating a world of possibilities for learning, rather than exclusively on planning specific activities.

This child-centred approach to planning has to take place in a warm atmosphere: the emotional environment.

● This emotional tone to any provision is created only partly through the physical environment. It depends heavily on how practitioners behave towards the children, their families and also to each other.

● Early years practitioners are able to create a welcoming environment, highly supportive of young children, in less than promising physical circumstances.

● In contrast, a physical environment that looks right for young children will not overcome adult behaviour that communicates a lack of interest, and a disengagement from young children's needs and interests.

Planning effort needs to go into the continuous provision of resources and areas in your indoor and outdoor environments – sometimes called the permanent play provision.

● The continuous provision aspect to planning links in closely with your thoughtfulness about the valuable experiences that should be available for children on a daily or very regular basis (page 10).

● Thoughtfulness about continuous provision involves using space and spaces as well as possible storage (page 34) and organising generous supplies of suitable open-ended resources (Rich et al, 2005, 2008).

Your indoor and outdoor environments do not remain the same forever. However, adults should have good reasons for making changes, if the change is not physically led by the children

Chances to be still and stare

themselves. Early years practitioners should not change corners or resources just for the sake of having something different. You need to reflect on 'Why am I considering this change?'. There needs to be a direct link into, 'What have I noticed about the children that makes me think this change would benefit them?'.

For well over a decade, the Early Excellence model (described in Marsden and Woodbridge, 2005) has focussed on using the skills of planning to create a learning environment that offers continuous provision to young children. Spaces are created and resourced in ways that enable even very young children to make active choices and organise how they want to play today. This approach is very different from an activity-led view of planning, in which practitioners organise and resource particular events for young children. You will find more about continuous and enhanced provision from page 35.

Feeling welcome and emotionally safe

In a warm emotional environment, even the very youngest children feel that they, and their interests or concerns, matter a great deal to their familiar adults. Early years provision of any kind works for the emotional wellbeing of young children when practitioners put their time and energy into personal interaction with babies, toddlers and children.

The physical environment matters but thoughtfulness about use of time, timing and supportive routines for any session or day is a vital contribution to planning for a warm emotional environment. Beginnings and ends to days are important because these are the transition times when children are welcomed to your provision and then waved a friendly goodbye. It is well worth thinking about the physical entry and exit points to your provision and planning for making these times supportive for children and families. A different approach is often needed, depending on whether children arrive and leave as individuals, or as part of one major entry and exit.

Babies and very young children need respectful attention to their personal routines of food, sleep, changing and playful interaction. But routines remain important for the over threes. The over threes also benefit from a flow to their day that makes sense to young children. Young boys and girls like some level of predictability, for instance knowing that snack or lunch time works in this way or that Tuesday is library day. Then they can

POINT FOR REFLECTION

Welcoming, cosy spaces

In terms of planning, a positive emotional environment is created through a physical environment that is welcoming and home-like. The best early years provision has been organised with young children in mind and enables them to feel that they belong here. Childminders should certainly not be thinking that they need to remove the homely qualities of what they offer, in order to replicate a classroom.

- Whatever your setting, your attention to the use of space, cosy corners, furnishings and use of materials helps young children to feel at home with you and other children.

- An environment needs to be interesting but not over-stimulating (either visually overstimulating from too much use of primary colours or aurally from constant background noise or adults who regularly call or shout across the room).

- Do you have places where young children like to linger? These may be the cosy corners, but young children often spend a lot of time in the bathroom, so this place needs to be welcoming and pleasant. In group settings, even more so than in a home, children often linger in the bathroom to have a chat with friends.

enjoy the unexpected and less familiar, which will include the adult-initiated special activities. Children cannot request an activity, such as large-scale mural painting, until they have experienced it at least once. Then they are able to ask to 'do big painting again'.

A warm emotional environment for a nursery, centre or your home as a childminder is largely determined by the behaviour of the adults; children follow your lead. No baby, toddler or young child will have their personal day improved by paperwork that has been completed mainly, or entirely, out of a sense of obligation to someone else. Their day will be improved by good quality interaction, made up from how you communicate with babies and young children and the ways in which you behave as a welcome play companion. Your time for alert observation,

Example: welcome time

Saying hello with the drum

Planning what to do first

At the time of my visit, most of the over-threes in Grove House Children's Centre attended for either the morning or the afternoon session. It was inevitable that the beginnings and ends of each session were a busy time of parents arriving or leaving. The team has found that children are more settled if their arrival is eased by joining their key group for a relaxed start to the session and a welcome to everyone.

Parents and children come through the main door to the nursery and divide to join the smaller key groups located in different spaces within the indoor environment. Children self register, with their parent if they want help, by finding the name card and placing it by the velcro fastening onto a large board (see page 12). The practitioner welcomes each child and parent by name and there is an opportunity for them to swap one book for another in their special Grove House borrowing/carrying bag. Families are welcome to borrow from the wide choice of story books and books about areas of interest that are part of the permanent provision in Grove House.

Children in each key group then sit in an informal, small circle with two adults, and any family member who is still settling

a child. An upturned tin acted as a drum and was passed around to one child at a time. He or she banged the drum while the others sang the 'Hello' song, welcoming children and all the adults by turn.

Children then had the chance to consider where they would like to start in terms of resources, from an array of images, and they left one or two at a time into the larger room or outdoors. Individual children then had the chance to consider what resources would be their first choice in play today. Their indoor and outdoor learning environment is full of possibilities and some children, especially in their early weeks of Nursery Class, can feel a little overwhelmed by choice. The Grove House team, like other practitioners with whom I have spoken, have noticed that young children often welcome a friendly thinking time to support 'Where shall I start?' In this Welcome Time the children were offered a set of images to support their choice. They then left this smaller room, one or two children at a time, to go into the main indoor spaces or to head outdoors.

Have you experienced children who appreciate some thinking time?

Example: relaxed communication with very young children

Kennet Day Nursery has a room which acts as a base for the very youngest children. In the base room I watched as a practitioner sat close to sitting babies and young toddlers. She was relaxed and took the opportunity simply to comment on some of what was happening at that moment. Some key points of her relaxed communication style were:

- She did not talk non-stop; her comments were for a reason. Sometimes she commented on a toddler's chosen play activity, such as "You're getting the bricks out" and "That's making a good noise".

- She was ready to play alongside as an equal play partner, showing by her actions how it was possible to fix bricks together. The toddlers could watch her and exercise free choice about whether to imitate.

- Another toddler was absorbed with looking at the photos that were fixed by velcro onto a stand. The practitioner commented briefly on the toddler's sequence with, "You're taking the picture off" then "And now you're putting them back on again". She offered help for the toddler to fulfil his intention.

- The mobile toddlers and twos were interested in the youngest baby in the room, who was five months old. They were careful and an adult was always close by. The toddlers liked to look at, touch and chat with the baby.

Example: planning around special events

Randolph Beresford Early Years Centre has an extensive outdoor area. The team have thought about different areas and small spaces, but have also planned for plenty of open space. This learning environment is fully used within a free-flow day. The centre has extended their use of the natural outdoors by weekly visits with small groups of children to their nearest public, large outdoor space in this urban area. This initiative has been developed by a team member who has completed Forest School training and has taken the role of coordinator for the centre.

The journey to and from the wooded copse is treated as an integral part of this special, regular experience. Children and their accompanying adults make a twenty minute walk along the same route to their outdoors base and then they catch a bus back for the return journey. They have documented both journeys as interesting in their own right - part of the whole outing - and created a wall display of photos and brief written explanations.

The practitioners aim to make the most of the wilder outdoors environment, However, they are also alert to building connections between experiences in the copse and back at the centre. Themes of great interest to the children have been building dens, using tools and bringing materials from the copse back to their garden. During the week of my visit the children were enthusiastic about building volcanoes in the centre garden – it was the time that the Iceland volcano was erupting in 2009. The plan shared with children was to take the resources for volcano making on their next trip to the copse.

It is striking that children themselves made direct connections between what happens in their woodland copse and back in the centre garden. They have thoroughly enjoyed easy access to mud in their wooded area and I watched two boys and one adult busy digging in the earth at the back of the centre garden. The adult was as interested as the children in what they found by their digging activities. The ground was quite dry and so they started to bring containers of water, filled from the outdoor tap in the centre of the garden. The dry area soon became damp, then very wet and then a muddy pool, which children and the adult worked to deepen. The adult suggested that it was time for them all to put on their wellingtons and the children cooperated. The experience then moved to serious mud pool splashing and other girls and boys joined in. The children themselves made the direct link to their outdoors trips with, "It's like at forest school" and they chanted, "Splash, splash" and "Splish, splash". The practitioner explained to me that children chant when they access the muddy sections of the copse.

and thoughtfulness over making sense of what you notice, pays off for children because what you learn influences what you then do. The impact may be almost immediate, in five minutes time, this afternoon, tomorrow or next week. This pattern of personal interaction and communication is led through the key person approach (Lindon, 2010c).

Planning and timing

All the teams from settings described in this book had thought a great deal about planning in terms of time and ensuring that children experienced a flow to the day and week.

- They had all organised for long uninterrupted periods for children to engage fully in experiences that interested them.

- Small group times were scheduled with care, not many within the day, and they happened for good reasons, which practitioners could explain.

- Thought had also been given to transition times, when young children needed to move from indoors to outdoors and in reverse, or between parts of a large building.

- In some places, timing and team work matters a great deal so that children could access the outdoors or have a relaxed meal time. Sometimes it would be impossible for all the children to be in the garden or eating lunch at the same time. Careful adult planning sat behind calm, unhurried movements of children over the day.

A growing recognition of the negative impact of outcome-led activity planning has led to greater use of the word 'experience'. This word is a more useful general term, because a great deal of child-initiated learning is broader than what is often meant by an 'activity', especially if that is only ever linked with 'play'. Children learn a great deal through play, but they do not exclusively learn through experiences that adults usually call 'play'. Children often want to help out within the domestic routines and they learn a great deal by happy involvement in meaningful events such as setting up for lunch and having their own job to do at tidy time. (See also the examples on page 57.)

Teams who have rethought their planning to highlight core or key experiences usually cover the importance of personal and domestic routines. A warm emotional environment places a strong value on nurture. Best early years practice

Planning is just as much about time and timing as the content of experiences or activities for young children.

- How many times in a day or session do you tidy up and re-organise the learning environment? Is it necessary to do a full tidy-up; can you do a minor tidy with the help of the children? What happens when young children are in the middle of play?

- Are children required to interrupt their self-chosen play to join in an adult-led activity? Valuable activities should be available throughout the day or session, and tomorrow or next week when children are enthusiastic and want to be involved or do it again.

Within the week, there may be special events that happen at a particular time or that involve moving children from place to place. The routines around such events need to be considered so that children are not rushed, but also to make the most of all aspects of a special regular event, such as the walk to the library.

Always think – does this timing work to benefit the children?

Keen to help

Example: a home-like feel and friendly routines

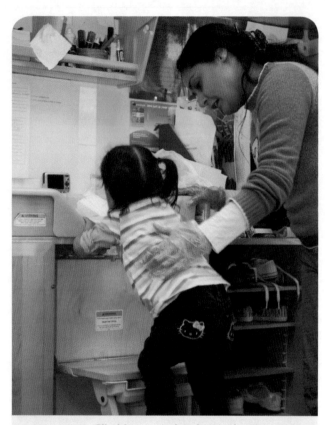

Climbing up to be changed

Enjoying lunch

1. Oakfield Nursery School

The nursery is located in a large house with four floors, including the basement level. The office and staff room is on the top floor. The approach to learning makes full use of the home-like atmosphere of the building.

The planning of the environment was deliberate in having some furniture which is that of an ordinary household – sofas, using the window areas for seating and large dressers in the communal areas. However, the physical environment is also resourced with child-sized seats, tables and storage facilities. The eldest children (four-year-olds) have their rooms on the first floor and by then are fully confident on the stairs. A sliding stair gate is available to use, if any child on this level has a disability that means they need an extra layer of safety. However, the normal pattern is that the stair gate is fixed open, unless there is good reason to slid the gate across and secure it. The wise approach has been taken that, by this age, children should have been given experiences that ensure they know how to behave safely on a staircase.

Plenty of time is allowed for when children are getting out into the garden and later back in again. These transition times are valued as times of learning. Children, other than those in the Baby Unit, need to negotiate a set of six steps from the main door to the garden level. It is one of the few times that young children in Oakfield are reminded to go one a time. This routine benefits from a friendly, informal queue, since it would be unsafe for children to head up or down in a rush. Babies and toddlers have their own set of steps from the lower ground floors where the Baby Unit is located. Toddlers are helped to manage those steps when their physical balance and upright mobility shows they are ready.

The whole nursery environment communicates a strong value about care, caring and enabling children to become active in their own personal routines. Planning and thoughtfulness about the learning environment definitely brings together 'care' and 'early education'. The bathrooms have been designed to be as light and pleasant as possible – babies, children and adults spend a lot of time in changing areas and bathrooms. From about 18 months of age to between 30-36 months, young children are part of the Toddlers & Tweenies rooms

Example: a home-like feel and friendly routines

within Oakfield. They have bathrooms that are organised for them to share in their own care – taps that are easy to work, soap dispensers, and privacy to go to the toilet, yet no chance of inadvertently locking themselves into a space.

The over-threes also have in their bathroom a series of discreet photos that remind young children of the sequence when they go to the toilet - from 'We pull our trousers down' through to 'We wash our hands' and 'We dry our hands'. Although adults are never far away, the objective is that threes are increasingly able to access and use the bathroom without much direct help and that fours will be comfortably independent in this important personal routine.

The nursery has a separate dining room, so staff do not have to reorganise rooms for snacks and lunch. Only the Baby Unit eats in their own space, in the lower ground floor. Again, careful planning over timing ensures that the dedicated dining room does not have more than one age group of children and their key persons at any one time. There is space for everyone, the conversational volume does not have to get high in order to be heard and children can sit in small groups at the tables.

Special events like dance that involve some changing of clothes are organised so that there is plenty of time. The getting ready for the activity and getting back afterwards into normal daily clothes are both planned as important parts of the sequence. The potential learning anticipated for these special events is not restricted to the dance or Stretch'n'Grow session itself. A high value is also placed on children's growing confidence to deal with their own dressing and undressing.

2. Grove House Children's Centre

In the Infant and Toddler Centre, babies and toddlers move freely between the base room for babies and the base for the toddlers. Both rooms have a raised changing area, with integral steps, so that the older toddlers can climb to the changing mat, with an adult beside them. The toddler section also has toilets with low doors for privacy, which are used by the eldest children who are toilet trained or in the process of reaching that point. Time is given for changing – never rushed – and this routine is treated as an opportunity for friendly conversation between a child and key person. There is also the chance for toddlers increasingly to share in their own care.

Babies and toddlers sleep when they are tired. The sleeping room with cots leads off the base room for the babies. Planning around personal routines develops from a close partnership with families, established from the earliest days, including a home visit, when families have chosen Grove House.

At lunchtime the toddlers sit at small tables and babies have their own low chair with integral tray. On the day of my visit, one practitioner made the point of smelling the aroma of the lunch before the dishes were visible. The twos had a guess at what was for lunch and one girl was correct in guessing that it was rice. The other guess of chicken was not right this time, as the second dish was revealed to be chickpeas and paneer cheese. An adult sits at each table to offer help as children need and key persons feed their babies, as well as providing a spoon for the baby to have a go.

Careful planning across the Children's Centre means that time and timing is considered. Children are not rushed from one part of the day to another. In the ITC I listened as a practitioner helped young children in the afternoon to think about "What's next?". Children thought that it was some kind of meal, but wrongly guessed lunchtime. The practitioner reminded them that they had had lunch and explained that the next event was tea time.

In the nursery class (3-5s) only a small number of children stay for the whole day, with lunch in the middle. They have lunch together as a social time. All the children have the opportunity to enjoy a snack within the morning or afternoon session. This routine is offered at a small table, with six to eight children at a time. Children can help themselves to water from a water cooler whenever they need a drink.

Think about your own planning, as a team or an individual practitioner. In what ways do you:

● Look at your learning environment with a view to creating a home-from-home atmosphere.

● Ensure enough time for personal routines like changing and shared routines like meals.

● Show parents that you value the preferences of their baby or child and work to create a personalised approach to nurturing children.

for young children is that practitioners continue to chip away at the artificial, but persistent, distinction that too many people still make between what they call 'care' and 'early education' (Lindon, 2006a and 2006b). Julia Manning-Morton and Maggie Thorp (2006) describe an approach to quality which focuses on making the most of opportunities for time with young children. The resource of Key Times looked at the many possibilities for close communication between familiar adults and individual children. The authors emphasised the importance of communication and interaction: that quality was not all about equipment and details of the physical environment. The resource focuses in particular on under threes and highlights the significance of actual times – routines which are important in the days of very young children - and places like toilets and bathrooms, where children spend a lot of time.

POINT FOR REFLECTION

Small as well as larger spaces

Perhaps you can recall from your own childhood how much children need and enjoy smaller, intimate spaces, that have a den-like quality. Can you remember, and describe, places where you felt safe and cosy? Where did you and your friends retreat to play quieter games, or just to relax?

You can create cosy corners with a welcome den-like quality in many different ways. I have visited nurseries who have used furniture, cushions and drapes. I have seen lightweight quilts laid over A-frames. Some settings have invested in the kind of large mosquito netting that is hung from a hook in the ceiling and designed to cover a bed. Practitioners have used simple tents – indoors and outside – as well as sometimes investing in more fixed outdoor shelters. But never underestimate the value of really large cardboard boxes, whenever you can get hold of some.

- What do you offer in terms of different sizes and types of spaces to the children in your provision?

- Have you created any small spaces which offer potential for the children themselves to embellish and make special?

- In what ways have you planned to have materials easily available so that children can entirely create their own cosy corners?

Continuous play provision

Every team or individual childminder has to work with the spaces available and make the most of what they have. You resource these spaces in ways that make sense for the age of the children and how they are likely to want to use rich, open-ended materials like water, construction materials including block play or small world resources. The details of this permanent play provision will not be identical across all early years settings but there will be some common features.

You consider the indoor and outdoor environment as a whole, rather than thinking that some areas of learning are only promoted indoors. Young children need generous amounts of time outdoors and practitioners need to resource the outdoor space with as much thought as the indoors. Your thoughtfulness and creativity over the physical environment is a vital part of planning.

- Look at the open space and smaller spaces you have and consider the routes between different resource areas or workshops. The same idea applies to outdoors – how do children move between different parts of your garden?

- If you have the full age range from babies or young toddlers up to young fives, you will need to consider indoor and outdoor spaces that are safe for the very youngest who spend a great deal of time on the floor or ground.

- Some settings will have dedicated home base rooms for different age groups, although there are advantages for all the children in mixing the ages for at least some of the day. However, small nurseries or home-based provision from childminders need to create spaces with a simple boundary where sitters and crawlers can explore.

- You have to work with the available physical space and fixed elements like doors, windows and built-in cupboards. But you will always have some choices, even when working with a physical environment that feels unpromising.

- Children need wider spaces in which to play their livelier games and build up some speed on occasion. In some settings this livelier play will mainly happen outdoors; it depends on your indoor spaces.

- But young children also delight in smaller spaces – indoors and outdoors – where they can play with one or two friends, snuggle up with a book or just chat and watch the world go by.

Different spaces and resources outdoors

Places to sit in peace

It works very well for children when you create areas that are resourced to support particular kinds of exploration and play. This way of planning and organising has been called a workshop approach or creating learning spaces. It is more usual now to talk about the permanent or continuous play provision. It does not matter what exactly you call this approach, so long as a team or individual practitioner views it as a major part of 'planning'.

The aim is to think and plan much more around important experiences for young children, supported by the resources in an accessible learning environment, than specific activities that adults have planned and resourced. There is definitely a positive role for well-chosen adult-initiated and maybe adult-led activities (Lindon, 2010d). But these opportunities rest on the backdrop of plenty of scope for children, even very young ones, to choose for themselves.

The approach of planning the permanent play provision is to gather together similar materials to establish areas (Marsden and Woodbridge, 2005). The Early Excellence model builds from what young children often want to do with these materials or particular equipment. Adults then resource this area in ways that will provide plenty of scope for child-led learning through play. This kind of planning depends on recognising that young children like to get their hands on materials, they are curious and want to explore and they need to be able to move – both themselves and interesting resources.

LINKS WITH YOUR PRACTICE

Sometimes it helps to track how children currently use the learning environment. Watch what happens in a typical session or day and consider planning changes on that basis.

- You do not, for instance, want to have a situation where, in order to reach the sink and wash up their paint pots, children have no option but to walk across the large mat where their peers are building important constructions.

- If you do not already, make sure that you spend considerable time at the eye level of babies, toddlers or children. What does the indoor and outdoor environment look like from the perspective of babies lying on their back or their stomach, a sitting toddler or a two or a four-year-old on the move?

- Are a considerable range of resources stored in a way and at a height that young children can see and choose baskets or individual items?

- Are some of the displays at the eye height of children? Some displays will be at adult height to engage parents.

For instance, most children love playing with water. Wise practitioners plan the availability of this natural resource to allow for the reality that children and the surrounding area will get wet. Useful planning then rests on what do young children often like to do with water. They like to do a lot of pouring, moving water around and putting items into the water. So children will appreciate and use a range of items that enable them to pour water, such as different sized jugs, funnels, tubing and sieves.

In a group setting, you may have a creative workshop (or another name which the children chose) where they can access a wide range of materials. If the materials include paint or even play dough, then it is wise to locate this area where you have a floor that is easy to wipe and a sink close by. Creative workshop areas can be established swiftly outdoors when materials are stored in containers that can be moved easily, especially if they are wheeled trolleys. In a small nursery,

LINKS WITH YOUR PRACTICE

Resources to support a particular indoor or outdoor area are best organised using a self-service format: either on open shelving or open containers close to the main play equipment.

So a water tray, trolley or other water resource needs a store from which children can select what they need. Some standing equipment have an integral storage area underneath. But you can place a storage container close by where children access the water. The water tray or bowl itself should not start out cluttered, because adults have put in specific items for their own purposes. In a welcoming learning environment children will fetch other items that they need.

In early provision where children's interests are respected, if there are polar bears and ice in the water tray, it will be because children want them there (see page 21). Polar bears will not appear exclusively because adults have decided that everyone is now going to do a topic on the North Pole. Even young children might become interested in creatures they cannot see in daily life. Wise practitioners build on a connection of interest. Perhaps young children talk with enthusiasm about the photos in a book, a nature programme they have watched on television, or they ask about small world size animals from zoo or farm sets.

A similar principle works with small role play. The basic equipment – a house or farm – can be out on the floor or table, if that is appropriate. Maybe you put out a few items but the main play accessories – little figures and furniture for the house, animals and fences for the farm – are available in a container by the main item. Help children if they want your assistance, or if their behaviour suggests to you that this play resource is unfamiliar. But do not, as part of your planning, set up everything in advance.

POINT FOR REFLECTION

Pretend play is not something to be 'managed'

Most young children love pretend play and the simple pretend of toddlers and twos develops into long sequences and flights of imagination.

You will most likely have a home corner, or other role play area that the children have established. However, it is not good early years practice for the adults to change a role play area exclusively on the basis of their own plans. Children should not come in on Monday morning to find that practitioners have demolished the pretend garage and replaced it with a vet's surgery, because the adults want to start a topic on 'people who help us'.

If children are enthused by what they learn from the vet who visits or the opportunity to go into the surgery, they will let you know what they want on their own. But it is just as likely that the dog who lives in the pretend garage gets sick and has to be treated – in an impromptu vet's surgery created with a large cardboard box and an official looking clipboard.

Early years practitioners should value pretend play as an important way in which young children learn and their power of thinking and imagination is released from the boundaries of what can actually happen. Threes and fours understand enough about the world to pretend to be somebody else and to undertake tasks that they could not in real life.

But the creativity of pretending is undermined if practitioners have been encouraged to view role play as something to be 'managed' through detailed planning about what children will pretend this week and what role play box they will use.

Example: children who can choose and organise

In Start Point Sholing a generous store of hollow wooden blocks enables children to build what and when they like. I watched Jamie (three years old) concentrate on building himself a wooden walkway across the room of the day nursery section of the centre.

Jamie persevered in selecting, carrying and positioning a whole series of blocks and was then able to walk along his construction, which was duly admired by the adults in the room. Jamie did not ask for any help, nor did he need any. However, he was able to plan and complete his construction project because the materials were easily available and there was a generous supply of blocks. Also the adults did not insist that Jamie's construction stayed in one corner. He built across part of the room in the day nursery area and everyone was perfectly able to move around him.

Later I watched Oliver, Jack and Ruby in the nursery class (3-5s) space. They were interested to make and draw Daleks. They had all the materials they wanted and could access them easily to resource their own chosen enterprise. A practitioner stayed by them and showed genuine interest in their different approaches to representing a Dalek.

Ruby wanted to paint and the boys to draw. Oliver was keen to explain the different parts of his Dalek as he drew and showed the practitioner which part was the shooter, which he also had in 3-D as a cardboard tube he was holding. The Start Point Sholing team take the line that pretend weaponry is treated like any other prop for imaginative play and accepted within this context. Oliver then decided that he needed to make a copy of his drawing and so he and the practitioner set off to make a photocopy, accompanied out of choice by Jack.

Look back over these examples and consider the issues they raise for personal reflection or discussion within a team:

● Jamie was able to build his wooden walkway across the room. Sometimes you may need to guide children that particular resources do not travel far from a given area. But are there times when opportunities to spread out are unnecessarily limited?

● Effective planning involves thoughtfulness about use of adults. In your setting are practitioners easily available to come alongside children's specific interests of the day?

Mark making at leisure

Storage that makes sense to young children

Easy for children to organise themselves

or your own home as a childminder, you can offer the same opportunities on a smaller scale.

Perhaps you have a mark making/emergent writing area. This is the main location for storing a wide range of mark making materials, paper, clipboards, and other stationery. There is space for children to organise themselves in that corner. However, mark making materials need to travel with children to where they need to use the items. Young children really benefit from experiencing that mark making, like counting, or measuring, is a skill that travels with them wherever they go in your setting. So, they need permission, and maybe a useful bag or container, to transport materials with them, including outdoors. Again, practitioners in a small nursery, or childminders in their family home, can offer the same opportunities. You will just have fewer containers in total than a large group setting.

It is appropriate, and wise, to involve children in tidying up and the clear understanding that everyone takes care of the shared materials, making sure they come back to the storage location, so someone else can find and enjoy them.

Planning an accessible learning environment for young children also means that you pay attention to how materials are stored. Look for storage systems, open shelving at child height with removable baskets and label any containers with

POINT FOR REFLECTION

Open-ended play resources

The aim is that young children have plenty of scope to access materials that can be used in different ways. Some bought play resources can be very useful but these need to be available alongside appropriate, safe, recycled materials, and natural resources from the outdoors (Hope, 2007; LEARN, 2002).

When you offer plenty of open-ended resources, babies and young children are able to make choices and determine their own explorations. However, the nature of the learning environment changes when it has been resourced mainly through bought single toys. Young children face a session or day dominated by waiting for a turn, giving up, or grabbing out of sheer frustration.

This unhappy situation is worsened when the purchase of toys has been weighted towards the moulded plastic variety, when no more than a couple of pairs of little hands can play with the toy at any one time. In contrast, several toddlers or children will be able to access and enjoy a basket full of soft scarves, large corks, little logs or plastic bottles each filled with something different (and with the lids screwed on tightly).

a photo as well as written words. If tools or other items have to be hung on hooks, then a photo or outline of the tool helps children to put the equipment back correctly and safely.

All settings do not have their own building; some nurseries and pre-schools operate on shared premises. Some groups have to set up at the beginning of every session and pack everything away at the end. This situation is less than ideal, but I have encountered many thoughtful teams who have not let this challenge cramp their style. Here are some thoughts for planning a positive learning environment under these circumstances.

- It would not feel welcoming for children and parents to be greeted by a bare room, but think again if you do all the setting up. There are benefits for children when you leave some jobs for them. They will feel a strong sense of belonging and respected as people who can choose.

- Consider working with children on a big room planner that helps everyone know what goes where. Young children are in the process of understanding the two-dimensional representation of a three-dimensional life. But the practical use of a plan can be supplemented with photos and other images of particular areas. Of course, this plan is not forever and can be reviewed in consultation with this group of children.

- Even two- and young three-year-olds can be active helpers because they know that, "We make our cosy den with the quilt and the big flowery cushions". You can say to children, "I started to set up our shop. But I bet you can decide what we need on the counter."

- Open, wheeled storage systems – that can also be locked down in place – are a good investment. So are baskets or other containers, that will fit easily into your cupboard or under-the-stage storage area, but which are light enough to be carried by one or two children as well as by an adult.

- It is unlikely to be possible to use wall displays to show children's explorations or ongoing projects. But large A3 size scrapbooks work well, and can be built up over time and brought out like any other valuable resource for children and parents to browse within the session. Laminated photos can be part of a resource area, made into a photo book, or using tough card can be made into a concertina screen with visuals.

- Again, consider involving children as much as possible in the tidying up at the end of a session or day. You and your colleagues may do the finishing touches, but the children can be involved in much of the task. Use this time to talk informally about tomorrow: what might be an extra for the construction area or what was missing from the dressing up basket.

- Some groups in shared premises have storage areas which are inaccessible to the children. One way around this challenge to enabling children to choose is to take photos of every kind of resource that is stored elsewhere. Make an Upstairs Cupboard Book with photos in a ringbinder system. Invite children to select a range from these resources each day for tomorrow and get then down ready for the next session.

Effective background planning about the learning environment by thoughtful practitioners means that young children can be active day by day in how they chose to access and organise the resources that are so easily available to them. Play and conversation become enjoyable experiences in which young children have considerable scope to use their own initiative. Practitioners are comfortable to share control with the children and welcome following the lead set by young boys and girls. In the settings I visited, there was a relaxed to-and fro between experiences genuinely initiated by children and those set in process by the adults – but for good reasons based on an ongoing close relationship with the children. Adults behaved as genuine partners in the play and were alert to what they could learn from this close involvement with the children.

Enhancing provision

Thoughtful planning creates an interesting and accessible indoor and outdoor environment: the permanent play provision. Observation-led short-term planning provides the reasons for enhancing that provision. You add resources for two main reasons: to support children's current interests or provision for interests which are predictable from what is currently happening.

You are observant of how children choose to use different areas of provision, equipment and resources. You listen to what they show you, but also to what they tell you they would like or what is not working very well at the moment. Valuable additions are usually not complex. For instance, at Start Point Sholing one practitioner told me how three toddlers in the later part of the afternoon of my visit had shown a persistent interest in climbing in and out of a frame in the garden that is used at other times for growing food. The adult plan for the next day

Example: outdoors in a large Children's Centre

Painting the stones

Using the pulleys

The Grove House team has made the most of the outdoor areas to the centre and the children and practitioners spend a considerable amount of time outside. The Nursery part (three to fives) of the centre has free flow for much of the day. The Infant and Toddler Centre (under-threes) have a modified free flow, adjusted to the fact that their youngest are not yet independently mobile. In both parts of the centre adults are out in the garden with children, coming alongside what children choose to enjoy from what is on offer.

The under-threes have their own outdoor area which is used for long periods of time through the day. Low level planters create a green boundary to one side as well as offering one source of outdoor seating. Steps, a small covered area and several large stone boulders also provide opportunities for children to sit if they wish with adults or other children. They have a large sand area and a fixed chalkboard, plus a selection of resources that are brought out in response to children's current interests. A marked track gives a focus for use of wheeled vehicles, while leaving a clear space in the middle. The under-threes team are alert to the current group of children and their motivation to be physically active.

The over–threes have a generous outdoor space, separate from the Infant and Toddler Centre. The Nursery garden has been organised into some dedicated spaces, such as a large, sunken area for sand, a digging area, raised mound with tunnel and slopes, a climbing wall and a choice of several covered seating areas. A circular track enabled energetic riding of bikes and a two-person vehicle. Children could access an outdoor tap to get water for their various enterprises. Another area has boundaries of low wooden palings and is full of stones and small rocks. Children can work with this resource in many ways and several metal containers on chain pulleys are fixed to one side of this space. On the day of my visit this space also had guttering and shallow trays (tuff spots).

Boys and girls had considerable freedom for active movement and also choose to settle in the various areas, including painting that was available under one of the covered areas. This art activity was resourced with an array of large stones and paint palettes. Children and an accompanying adult were busy painting their own rock. Towards the end of the morning and the afternoon sessions, some key groups gathered outdoors for a time of singing.

immediately became to gather large cardboard boxes. The aim was to offer opportunities so that these children, and any others who wished, could explore their climbing in and out, and any other uses they wished to make of the opportunities provided by the large boxes.

Some enhancements will be based on a reasonable prediction that children will be interested. For instance, at different times of the year celebrations will be visible in the local neighbourhood. For instance, your creative area could be enhanced with the materials to make Christmas cards or decorations. But the workshop would not be overwhelmed with Christmas paraphernalia. The arrival of a fun fair on the local common can provoke a great deal of interest from children about big wheels, spinning around or chatting about experiences which are a bit scary but still fun. You could put a couple of relevant books on obvious display but also be ready to listen and to provide recycled materials if some children want to make their own ride.

Your child-centred planning underpins decisions to offer specific adult-initiated and maybe also adult-led activities, that there is good reason to suppose will extend children's learning. Planned enhancements would also be visits within the local neighbourhood or inviting visitors to your provision. Successful local visits – perhaps to a park which you had not previously explored – could become a feature of your regular week.

Early years practitioners need to be observant: you look and you listen to what is going on around you day by day. You are alert to what has engaged children's hands and minds: you notice their actions, look at their face and gestures, hear their words and make sense of the meaningful utterances of babies and young toddlers that do not yet include recognisable words. Sometimes you capture what you notice in a written form that will add to a child's individual record. Sometimes you take a photo, but not all the time. However, your skills of observation should be switched on all the time, not only in response to a schedule of times to make a written observation. You then gain valuable feedback from children's words and actions about how well they are able to engage in the learning environment you have provided.

Enhancements can also be displays. The learning environment belongs to the children as well as the adults. In a joint enterprise with children, practitioners need to plan how best to make children's learning visible in ways that celebrate the journey of discovery or production, as well as the satisfactory end point.

Children feel a sense of belonging in their nursery, or your home as a childminder, when they can see that you have made space for what they want to collect and display. But young children also appreciate being involved in organising any kind of display – on the wall or elsewhere. Adult thoughtfulness about displays is as much a part of good quality planning

Example: different ways of using similar materials

In Oakfield Nursery School the outdoor area has been organised to offer open space for active movement, including wheeled vehicles, but also smaller spaces, seating areas and fixed resources like the sand. An area surrounded by a low fence has created a space free from bikes and high-speed movement.

During the day of my visit this enclosed area was equipped with slightly raised shapes and a sequence of equipment that enabled low-level balancing and moving between 'stepping stones'. The team anticipated that children would access this experience and the resource was enthusiastically used by all age groups throughout the day. The older children were very confident in their balancing and stepping from one raised section to the next. At one point the three- and four-year-olds

were keen to work with a balancing resource, that enabled children to stand on the flat section and rock from side to side using the curved base as they shifted their weight. Some children found this movement easier than others and an adult was close by to offer a hand if requested.

At another point in the day some individual toddlers were also very keen and able. I watched one eighteen month old girl who was very confident and, with a helping hand, did the whole run five times. The adult showed the same pleasure each time as the child when she triumphantly reached the end. Another girl (20 months) was less confident and needed more physical support and guidance about looking carefully where she placed her feet.

Example: observation-led enhancement of play provision

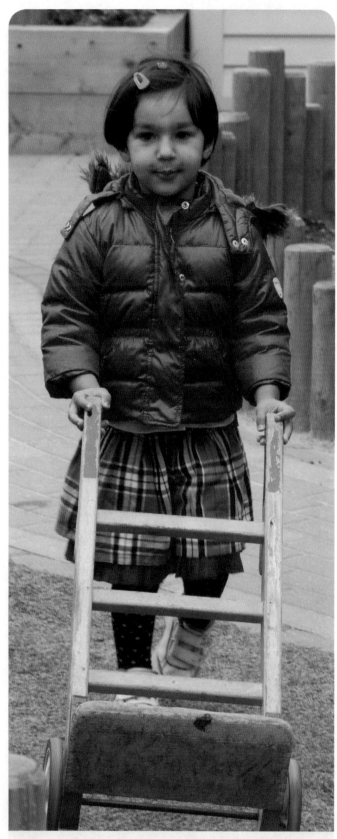
Using the trolley

The Grove House Nursery Class team have a daily afternoon planning meeting to reflect on children's spontaneous interests, as well as the two adult-led experiences that have been available. Here are a few highlights to show short-term planning that is so responsive to what has worked well today. See also the examples on page 51, 56 and 63. Observations and comments from the team led to immediate decisions, written down, for enhancements to provision, usually for the next day. Plans stretch into next week if a special event needs more planning time.

- My visit was on a Friday and the team were able to reflect on what happened on the single day within the week when there were no wheeled vehicles in the garden. This temporary absence seemed to create the opportunity for children to run races round the circuit that is usually occupied by children on one- and two-seater bikes. The conclusion was that a bike-free day could be a useful regular event.

- Practitioners had noticed that several children had been keen on using the trolley outdoors – the trolley was designed for adult-sized and designed for trundling stacked boxes. The children had been intrigued and had managed to move the trolley effectively around the garden. So the decision was that this trolley would be out again. Informal observation had confirmed that the trolley was safe to be out at the same time as the bikes; there had been no collisions.

- Several groups of children had been fully engaged in large scale chalking and drawing. Some thought was given to maybe moving some of the outdoor equipment and furniture to create more space for this enterprise. Practitioners had noticed that children especially liked painting with the sponges. Plans were made to offer more resources for large scale outdoor painting.

- A busy group had been pretend cooking in the sand for a sustained period of time. The decision was made to ensure next week that there were plenty of cooking items ready by the sand, to find the long handled wooden spoons or buy more if they could not be discovered.

- Another group of children had been intrigued by 'finding treasure' in another area of sand. The team decided that this possibility needed to keep running. The self-service tray by the sand resource had sieves and other items which could help in the treasure seeking.

Example: planning for the full possibilities of learning

The team of Grove House Children's Centre develop informative displays, with the help of children, which capture the story of enterprises, whether they last a day or longer.

The Nursery Class had a wide range of illustrated wall displays, including:

- A photo story of 'On the coach' provided illustrations and descriptive captions about a day out. The writing added to the photos in terms of what someone did or actually said, what was noticed and what happened.

- A special display showed 'Our home visits' in which children could see the photos that were taken when their key person visited them in the family home before children started at Grove House. Like other teams, Grove House offers home visits to families, most of whom accept this opportunity. The photos were close ups of the child and what they wanted to be captured on film, such as their bedroom or holding their special cuddly toy.

- Another wall display illustrated how, 'The children have been exploring textures while making play dough'. This display showed photos of children making and using their play dough, with a recipe provided. The lower part of the display featured 'What does it feel like?' with some words to describe texture – bumpy, rough, rubbery. Then the lowest part of the display had different materials fixed to the board that could be touched and felt.

In a similar way, wall displays in the Infant and Toddler Centre show babies, toddlers and twos in ways that enable their parents to share and understand what very young children have enjoyed. The displays are also of direct interest to children themselves and act a as visual reminder and focus of current interest, since most displays are set low, at child height.

- Displays showed how children choose from the accessible environment, for instance with 'Let's read together', showing babies, toddlers and twos enjoying books with an adult, and out of choice on their own.

- A long sequence of twenty photos and descriptive captions showed the story of 'When the chicks came to nursery' - the experience with real chicks enjoyed by the children and adults.

Photos can capture the moment

as the experiences that they document. A sequence of photos brings alive children's learning and makes visible the explorations, thinking and young problem solving that happened within that one-off or repeated event.

Large A3 scrapbooks are very practical, if you have limited wall space or cannot fix anything to a wall. Even if you have generous wall space, the large books or a photo album format are welcomed by children who like to browse them like any illustrated book. Ladybirds Pre-School creates records of shared events using photos and simple written accounts and places these books in a basket within the indoor book area. These stories of experiences shared by the whole group included an illustrated account of a visit by a fire fighter - the father of one of the children – and how he put on all his special clothes and equipment. Another book documented the enjoyable period of 'Snow at Ladybirds Pre-School'.

Wall displays or the large scrapbooks are designed to be used, not simply to sit there.

- Do watch out for whether mobile babies, toddlers and children choose to look at and touch any wall displays or book-style records.

- If there is limited spontaneous interest, check whether the placement of the display or scrapbook needs to be adjusted for easier access.

- Do the adults show an active interest in this material? Make sure that you and your colleagues look and touch and share your interest with children.

- There is no hard and fast rule about how long a display should remain on the wall or a scrapbook on a shelf. If children, and parents, are still keen to look and talk, then this resource is still 'live'.

- Review wall displays after a couple of months. It may be time to refresh the photos and written examples.

If all the children shown have moved on from your room or your provision as a whole, you would need a good reason to keep the display. One reason could be that this display or booklet is very successful in explaining your practice to families who are new to your provision.

KEY POINTS IN PLANNING THROUGH THE LEARNING ENVIRONMENT

Planning that pays off for young children includes significant attention paid to their learning environment.

- The emotional environment, or atmosphere, is just as important as the physical features and is led through the behaviour of practitioners.

- Children benefit from adult thoughtfulness about the timing of different events of a normal day and a positive approach to nurture and routines.

- The continuous play provision should offer generous resources for play, organised so that they are accessible appropriately for the age of children.

- Practitioners need to create cosy, as well as more open spaces, and gather equipment and resources into broad areas for ease of use.

- Babies and children need time and suitable spaces to explore and make active choices for their play and communication, both indoors and outdoors.

- The outdoor learning environment needs equal attention as indoors and young children need plenty of time in a well resourced outdoor space.

- Their learning environment is enhanced by additional resources and adult-initiated activities planned from knowledge of familiar babies and children.

- Practitioners need to share what, how and where young children learn with their parents – sometimes through visual displays of enjoyable experiences.

Chapter 3

Leading a thoughtful approach

Managers and other senior practitioners are responsible for guiding the early years team towards an approach to planning that genuinely supports young learning. Practitioners who usually work alone, such as childminders, can feel isolated over this kind of professional reflection. So, it is important to draw on available local support such as early years advisors with special responsibility for the childminding service and local networks.

Planning that supports active learners

Part of the senior role has to be a clear understanding of what is, and is not, required in the national early years framework that applies to your part of the UK. The national early years frameworks across the UK all expect that practitioners will exercise their skills of planning. The details vary between the four countries of the UK: the Early Years Foundation Stage (EYFS) in England (DCSF, 2008), the Foundation Phase in Wales (Welsh Assembly Government, 2008), the Curriculum in Excellence in Scotland (The Scottish Government, 2008) and the possibilities in the Early Years (0-6) Strategy in process in Northern Ireland (Department of Education, 2010).

Managers and senior practitioners have to become familiar with the early years framework that applies to them. The task is very often to be crystal clear about what is non-negotiable: the statutory part of any framework. These requirements are different from guidance: the part of a pack or additional publications that provide explanations, ideas, suggestions and maybe specific examples of practice. For instance, in England the EYFS main pack included both a statutory section and a guidance section, supplemented by the Principles into Practice cards. Many other booklets and CDs followed from the National Strategies team. These were all guidance documents, although they have sometimes been discussed as if everyone has to follow any suggested proforma for observation, recording and planning.

Within their different formats the different early years statutory frameworks have strands in common that apply to planning:

- The importance of learning through the medium of play within early childhood – with a balance between experiences planned by adults and children's self-chosen play.

- Planning by practitioners should pay close attention to the interests and current development of individual children.

- This observation-led planning should enable young children to stretch beyond their current skills and understanding, but should not impose unrealistic expectations.

- Forward planning should place equal value on all the areas of learning for development over early childhood, as they are described in this framework.

- Planning and evaluation of experiences should acknowledge how a positive experience for young children will support more than one area of learning.

Leading a team, or thinking deeply about your own practice, involves reflection around what these key strands mean and how some beliefs about planning could disrupt young learning. For instance, a positive focus on learning through play can be undermined by some interpretations of phrases much used in documents such as 'well planned play' or 'structured play'. The more adult-dominated approaches to planning risk imposing so much structure onto an alleged play activity that any playfulness has been organised out of the experience (Lindon, 2001 and 2010b). A developmentally appropriate interpretation of planning around play leads to experiences that familiar practitioners have organised on the basis of knowledge of these young children, who then enjoy this time.

It is never good early years practice when everything has been decided, by the adults, before children ever get their eyes and

Example: cutting and drawing

Cutting and making

A chance to draw with biros

In Grove House Infant and Toddler Centre three older toddlers and twos were enjoying a simple activity of cutting cereal boxes, occasionally squashing them as well, and adding strips of paper. They took breaks to chat and look at what the other children at the table had chosen to do.

The practitioner sitting with the children had planned this activity from her observations that some children wanted to cut with scissors but struggled with the skill. She had gathered the boxes because she knew some of the children could manage to cut card. She had cut some paper into strips beforehand, because the children found it difficult to cut whole sheets of paper. This adjustment enabled some children to feel a sense of achievement by cutting the strips, which could also be held taut by an adult. This example shows attention to appropriate next steps considered by an adult who knew the children well. She had prepared just enough to enable these young children to extend their skills.

On a table in the front room some twos were busy with large pieces of paper. They had crayons and biros but several children over the morning were most enthused about using

the biros. Young boys and girls focussed carefully, out of choice, and made a series of deliberate swirly marks, some of them tight spirals of repeated circling movements. Later in the day other children were drawing spiders and spidery shapes. They all held their biro with care and regularly stopped to look closely at what they had done before resuming this meaningful mark making. The children chose what to draw but adults were ready to admire what they managed. At one point a practitioner said, 'Fantastic' about a very detailed drawing done by a young boy and he repeated the word accurately – with a pleased expression on his face.

These very young children were able to select from resources made available on the basis of adult observations of existing skills. The children are secure within their learning journey towards literacy, in terms of making deliberate and meaningful marks. Appropriate next steps will be more opportunities like this, as well as the support from the children's learning environment which shows writing for a reason, along with visual material. There is good reason to predict that children will be fully confident in their skills of mark making by the time the abstract concept of written letters has begun to make sense to them.

hands on the experience. Over the last ten years or so, the conviction that planning meant fixed written plans imposed a rigid primary school lesson approach on far too many early years settings. Ironically, this unworkable system gained hold over the same period that some observers were challenging the consequences of inflexibility in the primary school curriculum.

The lesson plan approach has promoted the notion that it makes sense to determine in advance all the details of an activity for young children and attach firm predictions of what they will learn, so long as they complete the activity as directed by the adult. There are serious problems with this back-to-front approach, which some practitioners have encountered in their training as 'Design an activity to deliver this learning outcome …'.

- No matter how well you know young children, you cannot predict exactly what they will learn even from the most well-informed plan for an adult-initiated activity.

- You can have well-considered hopes, based on your knowledge of individual children, this group and this age range. You plan an adult-initiated (and maybe adult-led) activity with an open mind about several possibilities.

- However, the adult good guesses about what familiar young children might learn during and after this activity never ever become more important than what children's words and actions show you that they are most likely learning within an activity that is successful from their perspective.

- The lesson plan approach – whether it was called that or not – generated anxiety in some practitioners when young children were manifestly keen to learn in directions other than what was written on the activity planning sheet.

- The other serious problem was a misplaced belief that, if children were successfully persuaded to complete a given

Example: rethinking the approach to planning

The introduction of the EYFS (in England) has led many teams to revisit their views on planning, including what makes adult-led activities genuinely beneficial for young children. Well before the arrival of the EYFS, the head of Sun Hill Infants School and the team leader of the reception class (known as Year F) undertook a major exercise in reflection and changed the whole direction of practice, inspired by the Early Excellence model (page 31, also Marsden and Woodbridge, 2005).

- The Year F classes reorganised to work as one whole environment, with easily accessible resources available across the two indoor spaces and free flow for much of the day for children to access the outdoors spaces. The team worked as a whole to consider what should be available to children as continuous provision in the indoor and outdoor environments.

- The children were directly involved at the time of change, contributing their views about the detail of areas like construction, including the best name to call an area. Children in Year F continue to be active in adapting areas. Multi-purpose furniture and resources enables adults to be responsive to children's current interests.

- This provision was enhanced through additional resources, displays, organised visits and visitors to Sun Hill. Decisions about enhanced provision and experiences were in response to the children's interests, expressed in different ways and noticed because the team committed themselves to observation-led planning.

- Adult-directed activities no longer dominated the day for children. Instead, small group discussion times and adult-initiated/led individual or group activities were offered on the basis of observation of children's interests and needs.

- The weekly plan changed to have two Discovery Days each week when children's choice flowed throughout the day, with just two coming together times at the end of the morning and the afternoon. My visit lasted over this pair of days and I could see that the adults were very active as play and conversation partners.

- Within Discovery Days there are no adult-led activities. During the other three days of any week there are some small group times facilitated by an adult, such as active, hands-on maths activities with 5-6 children focussed on an adult-initiated task.

activity, they must have learned what was written in the outcomes section.

Overall the lesson plan approach prevented early years practitioners from making informed choices day by day, based on how children react. I encountered knowledgeable practitioners (not in any of the named settings in this book) who felt obliged to be dishonest. One instance was the ploy of writing the required learning outcomes in pencil on the activity planning sheet. Then these guesses were erased and pen used to write those skills which children had showed they were keen to practise and descriptions of what they had most likely learned. It then looked as if these points had all been successfully predicted in advance.

Highly anxious practitioners, and some managers, can feel reassured that they 'have a plan'. But serious problems arise for children's learning when uncertain practitioners believe they have to follow the written plan for the day in all the details, regardless of whether children seem at all interested. The consequence is that, even if children are enthusiastic about an adult-initiated activity, young boys and girls can be judged as 'off task' because they are keen to take this potentially interesting event in a direction not planned in advance by the adults.

There is plenty of support in official guidance documents across all early years frameworks in the UK that young children should be able to influence the direction of a play activity, or broader experience. There is no statutory requirement that practitioners impose their own structure in ways that refuse to share control with the children. A significant responsibility in leading a thoughtful approach to planning is to air those beliefs in the team that have led anyone to believe that they have to behave in this disruptive and unfriendly way towards young children.

There are serious negative consequences from planning that over-organises children's days and rests upon adult wariness about spontaneous play. Young boys and girls may be required to behave in passive ways and judged to be learning mainly, or only, if they are sitting 'nicely'. Leading a thoughtful approach on planning sometimes means that early years practitioners need to re-connect with the importance of lively physical activity for children and discuss openly the adult reservations about exuberant child-initiated games and general physical liveliness.

The significant review in Sun Hill Infants School overturned a very structured approach to planning, with adults in control of most decisions about resources and activities. Previously a proportion of the children, many of them boys, were regularly in trouble for being 'non-compliant' and 'off task'. Very soon after the Sun Hill team made the significant change to sharing control with the children, the 'behaviour problems' disappeared. Children were no longer expected to follow a programme in which they had no input. Differences of opinion or disinclination to cooperate became a reason to talk matters through, not evidence of misbehaviour.

The senior team of Kennet Day Nursery had observed a similar significant change when they re-organised their approach to planning to lead through children's expressed interests. In this setting, like Sun Hill, I saw young children – very young boys and girls at Kennet - were physically and mentally active in their chosen play and conversation. They could scarcely be 'off-task', because they were fully engaged with the adults in the nature and scope of any experiences. Young children were no longer required to move on a regular basis between adult-directed activities and spaces. So the times they came together with other children and an adult felt worthwhile (page 59).

Good practice on planning, like any other aspect of the work, is not to change approach so often that the team can never settle into a new way of working. However, young children are well supported by early years practitioners who are willing to reflect on their approach and make further changes for good reasons.

The approach to planning in Garfield Reception Class had been the result of rethinking by the reception team and the head of the Children's Centre which shared the site with the school. They had already been planning each following week through the expressed interests of the children. But the team had observed that taking a largely 'next week' approach mean that sometimes what they planned as adults no longer fitted what children were keen to do – their interests had further evolved even over a couple of days.

The reception team changed to planning with children on a 'today' basis through three focus children each week. The detailed planning for those days is led by the interests of the focus children and their chosen enterprises usually involve other children, as well as an adult (examples in Lindon, 2010d). At the time of my visit, the reception team had been using this modified method of following children's interests for nearly a year. They had found that the change enabled them to focus much more closely on children's motivation to extend their knowledge or skills in particular directions.

Example: fine tuning your approach to planning

Children need time to focus and practise

The approach to planning in Garfield Reception Class had been the result of rethinking by the reception team and the head of the Children's Centre which shared the site with the school. They had already been planning each following week through the expressed interests of the children. But the team had observed that taking a largely 'next week' approach mean that sometimes what they planned as adults no longer fitted what children were keen to do – their interests had further evolved even over a couple of days.

The reception team changed to planning with children on a 'today' basis through three focus children each week. The detailed planning for those days is led by the interests of the focus children and their chosen enterprises usually involve other children, as well as an adult (examples in Lindon, 2010d). At the time of my visit, the reception team had been using this modified method of following children's interests for nearly a year. They had found that the change enabled them to focus much more closely on children's motivation to extend their knowledge or skills in particular directions.

Before the fine tuning of their approach, the Garfield team had continued to plan additional adult-initiated or led activities. They recognised that too many of these plans were more about filling boxes on a planning sheet than reflecting a close connection with what children were poised to explore and enthusiastic to learn. With a closer look, some of these planned activities were too ambitious for the current skills of the four- and five-year-olds, or failed to involve children on the day.

Even experienced practitioners could feel a sense of obligation to carry on with an activity because it was on the planner. Removing this aspect to planning in reception meant that the team was freed up to respond swiftly to the expressed interests of any children, not only the three focus individuals. The team was aware that spontaneous conversations and play were the best opportunities for sustained shared thinking.

Even with a strong focus on children's interests are you still planning more adult-led activities than is justified by the observable benefit to the children?

Leading a thoughtful approach

Time for everyone to have a go

In their own personal style

Before the fine tuning of their approach, the Garfield team had continued to plan additional adult-initiated or led activities. They recognised that too many of these plans were more about filling boxes on a planning sheet than reflecting a close connection with what children were poised to explore and enthusiastic to learn. With a closer look, some of these planned activities were too ambitious for the current skills of the four- and five-year-olds, or failed to involve children on the day.

Even experienced practitioners could feel a sense of obligation to carry on with an activity because it was on the planner. Removing this aspect to planning in reception meant that the team was freed up to respond swiftly to the expressed interests of any children, not only the three focus individuals. The team was aware that spontaneous conversations and play were the best opportunities for sustained shared thinking.

Each national framework for supporting early years practice places a clear value on physical development as an important area of learning and recognises that early childhood is a crucial time to encourage healthy habits of exercise, as well as food leading drink. One of the many negative effects of top-down pressure on early years practice has been a rigid sit-down-and-concentrate definition of what counted as 'proper' learning. Such an outlook brings unrealistic expectations that young children should be able to remain still for long periods. There

is also often the misguided perspective that learning worthy of respect only happens indoors, probably led by an adult, at a table or with children sitting quietly on a mat.

Sadly, children's natural exuberance then becomes seen as an inconvenience to the smooth running of the day.

● Thoughtful discussion within a team sometimes needs to address questions like: "Why do we think this is a problem?" and "Why are we trying to plan liveliness out of the day or contain it within very limited times?"

● Children need to be active learners and sometimes that means physically active: moving themselves and important resources around the learning environment.

● An excessively intellectual, classroom view of how to promote literacy skills has also ignored the vital role of physical dexterity and large scale meaningful mark making. Developmentally appropriate planning by teams and individual practitioners ensures that opportunities for using early literacy skills are spread throughout the indoor and outdoor environment.

In recent years adult anxiety has grown about the health risks of inactivity and how to provoke children out of being sedentary.

The response has then sometimes been to promote very structured programmes of adult-led physical activities. It is seriously unwise to respond to this legitimate concern about developing healthy habits in early childhood by planning the play out of physical activity. Young children are naturally active; it takes serious adult discouragement and an unfavourable learning environment to stop them.

Young children need and want plenty of time outdoors, with suitable resources and the chance to be physically busy, manage their own risk and have adventures – see the example below from Kennet Day Nursery. They also benefit from some adult-initiated and maybe adult-led opportunities for special activities – see the example that follows from Oakfield Nursery School.

Observation-led planning

Reflective discussion around the subject of planning, observation and assessment makes an important distinction between 'planning for learning' and 'planning of learning'. Changing a single word makes a world of difference here.

- An outlook of 'planning for learning' should mean that early years practitioners focus on the possibilities and opportunities for young children to learn. This open-ended approach weaves in your general knowledge of child development with your specific knowledge of individual babies, toddlers and children.

- In contrast, an approach dominated by 'planning of learning' rests on the mistaken belief that it is appropriate – or even possible - to identify in advance the details of what children will learn if they complete this given activity (see also page 68).

Planning for learning means that you entertain well-supported hopes for what familiar children could well gain from an experience that you judge they are unlikely to request or organise for themselves. You can have a clearly expressed adult intention to open a door of knowledge and experience for young children. You plan for encouraging circumstances so that they want to walk through that door.

This approach provides a secure basis for looking at children's developmental progression, using the resources that are part of each early years framework across the UK. In the EYFS for England the early learning goals (ELGs) are for the end of the stage, five-year-olds in reception class. So practitioners who

spend their days with children younger than this age have to think always in terms of 'towards' a given ELG.

For instance, one of the ELGs at the end of the Numbers as Labels and for Counting strand in Problem Solving Reasoning and

LINKS WITH YOUR PRACTICE

The example from Kennet Day Nursery highlights the important aspect of planning for best use of the adults in your provision. Kennet, like several other settings I visited for this book, had organised to run a free-flow indoor-outdoor approach for the over threes. (The under threes had generous time outdoors.)

Planning for organisation of the staff means that practitioners need to work with a team ethos. A key person approach (Lindon, 2010c) ensures that young children form a close, affectionate relationship with a familiar adult. Planning for timing and routines within a day or session enables children to spend relaxed time in their small key group. But for significant amounts of the day or session children are able to move freely.

- I watched in Kennet and the other settings as all the practitioners kept alert to the flow of children. A brief look or words would pass between colleagues as one person moved towards an area where a group of children might welcome an adult play companion.

- Forward planning for deployment of the team usually meant that everyone knew who would be based inside today – so children who chose to spend time indoors always had a companion.

- In those settings with a large outdoor space, forward planning allowed for a minimum number of named team members who would be based outdoors today and spread through the different areas.

The practitioners were not rooted to the spot and there was a sense of shared responsibility – not a 'my patch – your patch'. It was easy for someone to ask for support, such as keeping an alert eye because the first practitioner needed to take a child inside for personal attention such as toileting or a minor accident.

Leading a thoughtful approach

Example: a welcome for physical play

Time to enjoy outdoor activity

1. Physically active exploration

Planning in Kennet Day Nursery means that all the children have generous time outdoors and the three- and four-year-olds are able to have free flow between their indoor space and the garden. The garden has different areas and the main section has a slope, part of which is clear of any fixed equipment. Some children, including a few of the older two-year-olds, are adept at riding and coasting a bike down the slope at speed. The adults keep a watchful eye but do not intervene, unless they judge that a child is not fully aware of another child or temporary obstacle in their path. The children are skilled at steering, use their feet flat on the ground to brake, but they are also adept at steering into the earth for additional braking power.

Children use the opportunity of the slope for sending down small toy trucks and following on foot and running down. They put in serious physical effort to get back up the slope many times, carrying their truck or pushing and pulling their chosen wheeled vehicle. Another favourite activity is for the threes and fours to push the tyres up to the top of the slope and let them roll down. They understand that

this activity does not happen when any of the twos are in their garden, since these younger children are not adept at getting out of the way.

Threes, fours and some older twos are physically very active. I watched as they chose to work hard at their skills of balance on the low sections of fixed climbing equipment, held their balance on the wobbly bridge and in some cases succeeded with a challenging climb into the hanging tyres and between more than one tyre.

One absorbing activity lasted all day in different formats. A substantial store of hollow wooden blocks are kept in an outdoor store. In the morning one boy asked a practitioner for help in opening up the store and getting out the blocks. Soon the boy had moved most of the blocks out of the store and was building with them just outside. The practitioner was by then sitting on a pile of blocks in the storage facility, with the top up and the doors open, chatting with the boy.

The blocks remained out all day and at the beginning of the afternoon several children – three- and four-year-olds - had

Example: a welcome for physical play

been hard at work creating a substantial construction with a raised walkway of blocks, partly one block high but with a higher section that was three blocks high. The middle of the long construction was a sloped section designed for climbing up and over. The children built this to their own design. The only practitioner input was to ensure that the blocks were safely aligned and to realign them if they shifted.

When the construction was complete, many children were keen to have a go, willing to wait their turn patiently. They asked for help, if they needed it, from the practitioner who based herself by the challenging sloped section. This child-initiated activity ran for most of the afternoon. At one point there were five children standing on one section of the raised walkway and a practitioner was throwing a ball to each child in turn, calling their name first. At another time individual children decided on the height from which they felt comfortable to free jump, once or twice indicating that they wanted to jump into the arms of an adult.

This construction was built close to the storage facility. But I was told that children move the blocks all over the garden. In recent weeks, a group of boys had wanted to build a wall at the top end of the garden and persevered in carrying a considerable number of the hollow wooden blocks up the slope and had built their wooden wall across the width of the garden.

2. Special physical activities

Children in Oakfield Nursery School have plenty of time outdoors when they choose what they play, with whom and with what resources. However, the week also includes some experiences offered by specialists who visit the nursery on a predictable basis. These special times for the over threes include a football and general ball skills session, dance, baking and Stretch'n'Grow (an exercise session using energetic and lively music).

Wall displays document these special times, with photographs and practical captions which describe what children gain. The display of 'Here are some of the things we learn in our football sessions' has many photos of active children with captions like 'Bounce a ball', 'Have good balance' and 'Run fast'.

A recent change in the pattern of the football session reflects the Oakfield commitment to listen to children. A while ago, the team invited the children to express their

views about their special football sessions. Children used smiley, turned up faces and less happy turned down faces. Most of the comments were supported by the smiley faces. So practitioners asked children to say a bit more about what provoked the turned down faces.

The children were clear that it was less enjoyable if they had to wait a long time for their turn. They gave the example of the way that kicking a ball at the net was organised at that point. The adults listened and talked with the specialist who organises the football sessions. He found an easy alternative that involved more of the movable nets that are used in this special session. He also revisited other activities to reduce waiting time as much as possible. The children were pleased with this change.

- Are you providing generous opportunities for children to be physically active and fine tune their skills within child-initiated as well as adult-led activities?

- Young children often have ideas for how an experience could be 'better'. Do you invite their views?

Purposeful physical effort

Numeracy is 'Recognise numerals 1 to 9'. (Despite the belief of many practitioners, there is no Early Learning Goal expecting five-year-olds to be able to write any numbers.) Practitioners working in a reception class would be observant of the skills that children already have in terms of showing their understanding of the abstract symbols of written number. Planning should include attention to the learning environment: can children see numbers that are placed for good reasons and do they spontaneously use number language? Do children pick up number cards or plastic numbers for their own use? But it would also make sound developmental sense to offer games that enable children to recognise the actual number as well as count up to a given number. Local trips can be good opportunities to go number spotting.

Some fours will be ready for the activities mentioned above. Have you observed how some children in their pretend shop are on their way towards recognising some numbers and using the correct words? Do they show you that they are beginning to grasp that the symbols of number are a different set to the symbols of letters? On the basis of observation you can make informed decisions about appropriate adult-initiated activities.

However, practitioners who work with threes or twos – let alone the under twos – cannot plan in line with this Early Learning Goal. Sensible planning for early mathematical learning has to rest upon a clear view of what young children need to experience and understand before written numbers will make any sense to them at all. Supporting materials, for instance the relevant Development Matters column of the EYFS Guidance (2008), help less sure practitioners to think and discuss around what it looks like when very young children are on the learning journey towards numeracy.

It is important to know and recall that the EYFS Development Matters columns were not created as a developmental tracking instrument. They are descriptive items, loosely linked with age bands, that were developed backwards from the early learning goals established for the 3-5 Foundation Stage guidance – and which passed scarcely unchanged into the 0-5 EYFS. Part of leading a positive approach to planning is to help practitioners use any of this material in a thoughtful way.

In terms of observation-led planning, early years practitioners are not obliged to look for exactly, or only, what is written in the Development Matters columns. However, some of the material offered a useful starting point. For instance going back to the numeracy example, practitioners involved with younger children look out for threes who are able to count items, twos who are interested in amount through 'lots', 'more', or 'not enough'

POINT FOR REFLECTION

Learning from an observation

Alert observation should help practitioners to understand how an experience has unfolded for the children. Observation will usually, and should, tell you something you do not know already.

Adult observation of young children should enable you to learn about what has interested this child, or small group, what they chose to do and what they have probably learned. From there you move on to plan a well-informed, developmentally sensible next steps for enhanced provision or experiences to offer.

The value of observation is lost if an approach to planning has convinced practitioners that the goal of observation is to confirm what was predicted within the outcomes section of the planning format.

It is worth saying again: observation-led planning is all about adults learning more about the children in their care, and not about confirming the delivery of predicted outcomes.

and toddlers and even babies who show surprise that an item has gone missing from an array of items or an extra one has appeared. It is then feasible to make the most of very young children's grasp of amount as they organise and re-organise their collection of stones or show immediate interest when you start a nursery rhyme that involves counting up and down.

Team leaders sometimes have to rebuild confidence in one or more practitioners who have become anxious about any approach to planning that deviates from pre-written lesson plans for adult-led group activities. Managers need to be honest, if only with themselves, when they are uneasy about trusting the power of play and an adult alert ear and eye on each day. Part of this professional turnaround is to reconnect with what 'planning' has to mean if adult plans offer a genuine support to young learning – what was discussed in the first section of this book.

The related professional understanding is about observation, assessment and planning as part of an ongoing cycle, in which practitioners learn – if necessary – to tolerate the uncertainty

Example: playing with Unifix blocks

Unifix in the morning

Unifix in the afternoon

The Grove House Nursery Class team introduces a small number of adult-initiated activities within any day. Any resources are provided for reasons that connect with children's current skills and the team considers 'what next' on the basis of what children actually do with the materials.

On the day of my visit, one table was resourced for both half-day sessions with a large array of different coloured Unifix blocks along with the trays, grids and different base sheets. Children gravitated towards this table throughout the morning and the afternoon and they were welcome to explore different uses of the materials. Some children never came to the table and there was no obligation for any child to spend time here. Practitioners were deployed throughout the indoor and outdoor spaces and were involved in the many other experiences that had caught children's attention and energy.

The morning group was especially interested in matching single blocks to the coloured squares in the base sheet. The adult sitting with them followed the children's interest and commented on their searching and matching activity.

In contrast, the afternoon group became most interested in building tall towers with single cubes. The practitioner in the afternoon – a different adult - was equally interested by the challenge these children set themselves of building tall structures no wider than a single block. They were keen to build but also to talk about the height and look closely at the unstable nature of some of their taller towers.

In the end of day planning meeting practitioners discussed how children had used the Unifix cubes. The team had not anticipated that some children would so enjoy their ability to choose a different base sheet. It was agreed that this resource should become a more permanent addition to the resources, so that children could self select. An additional idea was that rulers should be added to the Unifix resource, because some children were so intrigued by the towers they built and their height. Children in the nearby construction area had also been busy measuring blocks and cubes – so a sustained interest in measurement could be supported.

Do you have examples of when children choose to use the same basic resources in different ways?

Example: letting children lead the play

A spontaneous dancing time

In Grove House Children's Centre the team planning across the whole provision demonstrates a shared commitment that everyone is very responsive to what children want to do right now.

In the outdoors area for the under-threes the practitioners responded swiftly to requests from children by words or indicated by a child's actions. At one point several twos and toddlers were with two adults hanging on tight to a large hula hoop and enjoying impromptu singing of *Ring-Ring-a-Roses* and then *Here We Go Round the Mulberry Bush*. The hoop kept everyone easily in the circle as they moved around.

The organisation of the indoor spaces for under-threes has a range of cosy corners and slightly more open areas. At one point two toddlers in the front space of the twos home base room started a spontaneous dance to the background music. Very soon a small group of toddlers and twos were dancing and one adult joined in with them and then another. The dancing session continued for a while and then two practitioners offered for children to be swayed in a large piece of material. The cloth was placed on the ground, a child lay on it and then the adults gently swung the child from side to side with the material creating a hammock shape. Other twos and toddlers held a bit of the cloth and everyone sung a special song, featuring the name of the child each time. At the end of the song, this child was gently lowered to the floor and their place taken by the next child.

Later in the afternoon an adult responded to the spontaneous event of a young girl realising, "Where's my slipper?" She had on only one slipper and one bare foot. A search began and a boy came up with what certainly looked like the missing slipper. The adult took the opportunity to compare this slipper carefully with the one still on the girl's foot. They all agreed that the slipper looked the same – it was the same style – but they found that one slipper was definitely smaller than the match they were seeking. The boy was still thanked for his find and in a short while the actual missing slipper was discovered.

In your team, is everyone ready to flow with the small details of children's interests?

of real learning through play, and other important experiences which the children themselves probably would not call 'play'. A key point about developmentally appropriate planning over early childhood is that the approach you build with your team has to leave everyone confident to seize the moment when even very young children lead and you follow. Planning has gone seriously awry if the end result has been to plan out spontaneous play.

POINT FOR REFLECTION

Facts and well-supported opinions

Observations that enable practitioners to make a difference for young children have to be a combination of fact and supported opinion. Some early years practitioners are still being told that observations must be exclusively factual and not include any opinions. If practitioners followed this direction they might have full descriptions of what happened, what was said and done. But there would be no element of the crucial 'so what?' that leads you to well-informed, short-term plans about next steps.

Look at the example on page 51 about the Unifix bricks. The practitioners directly involved in that experience were able to describe during the team meeting what individual children had chosen to do with the materials. But if the discussion had stopped at that point, there would have been no forward plan for enhancing this experience.

Managers and other senior team members need to grasp what exactly staff have been told in their initial training, or on subsequent training days. Sometimes the 'give facts and not opinions' firm advice is aimed at preventing unsupported statements such as 'Terry has poor language' or 'the children showed good social skills during key group time'. This less good practice needs to be challenged in a firm but friendly way with "What leads you to say that Terry's language is 'poor'?" or "Can you give me an example of what you call 'good social skills' from these four-year-olds?"

But young children's learning will not be well supported if any of your staff believe that they must not express opinions. An observation should be a careful combination of 'What were the children doing?' with 'What does this tell me?'

LINKS WITH YOUR PRACTICE

Close observation of familiar young children lets you make an informed assessment – a judgement – about possible next steps of learning for individuals and small groups with sustained shared interests. The "what are the next steps?" question needs to have the firm foundation of 'what is this child or small group of friends doing at the moment?' This question often divides two parts:

● What resources or equipment have babies or young children chosen to use?

● What have they chosen to do with the materials?

You make the positive difference for young learners by observing the answer to those two questions, supporting children in their current enterprise (which may be admiring rather than always being directly involved) and by enabling them to extend what they are currently keen to repeat, with their own slight variations.

Practitioners who have been given an activity-led perspective on planning sometimes think the main point is that young children should be doing something different. If toddlers have spent much of today filling and emptying their buckets in the sand, sensible next steps will not be to get them to spend time tomorrow with some jigsaws. If tomorrow morning one or more toddlers head for the accessible shelf where you store jigsaws, that is their choice.

Observation-linked next steps need be connected with the kind of resource children have selected and the kind of actions they chose to make. In this case, next steps will be connected with sand, or maybe other natural materials and enhanced provision for filling and emptying. The enhancements could also offer scope for piling up and knocking down and the ability to move materials around the environment.

Some practitioners – maybe some of your own staff group – are less sure about following children's interests when very young boys and girls are not yet able to express those interests in spoken words. But babies and toddlers show you very clearly by what they do and attempt to do. Look at the example about cutting and drawing on page 42, or the opportunities for clambering on page 4 – some literal next steps.

Being observant

Being observant is supported by making some planned observations, often led by an agreed focus on one or two key children per week (page 16). But informal observations matter just as much as planned sitting with your notepad and camera. Practitioners in all the settings described in this book were ready to notice, and sometimes make a written note of what happened in front of them. Assessment basically means making sense of what you have observed – brief events as much as long, sustained sequences.

● So what? What happened, what do you think was important for the children and what did they learn?

● With an adult-initiated activity you may have looked ahead to consider what these children might learn, perhaps what you hoped they would gain.

● But the most interesting assessment now is what actually happened – how did they use the resources that you made available, what interested them most.

● On reflection now what do you think the children most likely learnt, what have they shown or said to you?

● These questions and this kind of discussion are all part of reflective practice (Lindon, 2010b).

Observation-led planning, with the intervening thoughtfulness about 'so what?', enables practitioners to consider well-supported next steps for individual children or small groups who enjoy being together. Practitioners, led through the key person system, have a sound grasp of the learning journey of their key children. During my visits to settings I take time to ask about and listen to what I call the 'back story' to what I observe during the hours I spend with children and practitioners. I enjoy these conversations with practitioners, often the child's key person, as they share with me the highlights of an individual learning journey, or one shared for several young children who have created a shared enterprise. You can read examples in this book on page 60 and more in Lindon (2010c) or the learning stories in Rich et al (2005, 2008).

Careful observation of children also means that practitioners, led usually by the key person, will have a well-informed view of what they could introduce to young boys and girls that the children do not yet have the experience to request. There is a strong focus in early years frameworks across the UK on plenty of time for child-initiated experiences. The aim is for a balance between these opportunities and adults sharing their greater knowledge and experience wisely with young children. Thoughtful adults should be providing first-hand experiences that are authentic and genuinely extend the understanding of young children. I fully agree that young children learn a very great deal through play. But many valuable experiences are more real life than play; they are the under-fives version of life skills.

Support for what a child wants to do

Time to support practical skills

Example: observation-led planning

In Oakfield Nursery School the personal records for individual children build within a large A4 ring binder. Spontaneous as well as planned observations are captured by photos and descriptive, written comments. Observations cover the wide range of play and conversational experiences. But the team also value nurture, and children's learning journey towards self-care and independence in the broadest sense. When time is put aside for a planned observation, it may be of a child-initiated experience. Or else some observations are made of a child's response to a resource introduced by the adult or a small group activity which this child has joined.

Any observation includes both the description of 'what happened?' and an informed making sense by the key person of what the observation shows about this baby or child. This evaluation is cross-referenced as appropriate to the six areas of learning within the Early Years Foundation Stage. The 'next steps' part of observation-led planning is connected fully with what the practitioner has learned from this observation, to add to her current knowledge of key children.

In the two groups of over-threes individual observations are also made over time which document how children respond to resources especially supportive of aspects of learning within Problem Solving, Reasoning and Numeracy and also in Communication, Language and Literacy. So, for instance, if a child is interested in playing a board game, the key person can access a photocopied sheet which has an image of the board game, and an open-ended description of what a child might learn from playing the game.

The sheet is then used in a personal way for the key person to note what this individual child actually did in the game, playing with another child or with an adult. The observation captures what the child understood and what was confusing, linking into 'what next?'. It is highly likely that children will choose to play with the board game again in the future. The key person can then add this to the record, with a new date, and document how this child's grasp of the game, and the underlying mathematical understanding, has progressed.

In what ways do you capture the individual responses of children?

Planned group times

Young children, who know each other and are comfortable together, may enjoy small group come-together times.

Thoughtful teams discuss:

- What experiences will work well in small group times? What leads us to believe that this kind of experience will work better when a group comes together than if we offer it as an open-ended activity?

- When are the best times for coming together in a group within the session or day?

- How big is the group – what works for the children? This decision should never be that life is easier for the adults if children are brought together in a group at this time.

- Babies, toddlers and twos do not appreciate being organised into group activities as such. They certainly should not be expected to sit quietly and take turns in speaking. They will appreciate intimate come-together times through their key group.

- What do you do in the group, what do you hope this time will offer to the children? How do you observe and assess whether it is working well?

- If one or more children are loath to cooperate in this group time, do you allow for the real possibility that there is something wrong with your planning rather than with the children?

There is no requirement from any of the early years frameworks across the UK that settings have to organise a given number of group times, or any at all. Certainly it is unwise to think that

Example: first-hand experiences

Making sandwiches

1. Making real sandwiches

In Grove House Nursery Class, I watched as one practitioner took responsibility for an adult-led activity of making sandwiches. She remained seated with the children throughout and created a relaxed atmosphere in which children looked, listened, made decisions and created the sandwiches of their choice.

The table took a maximum of six children, so the practitioner was able to be close and give individuals her full attention. However, this opportunity was available throughout the morning session and then again in the afternoon session. Many children were able to opt for this activity, without any sense of time pressure.

Each child had their own chopping board and knife. A cheese grater passed around as needed. The practitioner invited children to start by "Having a look at what we've got". She named all the ingredients: bread, butter, cheese, cucumber, pepper, tomato, and onion. She also pointed out the implements they could use. Children were keen to smell the ingredients, including the raw onion which provoked

some surprise, and to taste small amounts. They were intrigued by the layers of the onion and finding out about the inside of a tomato.

These three- to five-year-olds wanted to be engaged in every part of the experience: looking at and smelling the potential ingredients, spreading the butter, cutting up their preferred items, grating the cheese, making their sandwich, and wrapping it in foil to take home if they did not want to eat it straightaway. Children then made their own name label to go with any packages that needed to be stored, ready for home time at each session of the day.

The practitioner gave the same full experience as a new small group formed, or as individuals completed their sandwich and others joined. Some children came close to look before deciding to take up a place at the table. The practitioner invited them to watch and asked, "What do you think we're doing?".

The knives had a serrated edge – not over sharp – but some children needed guidance to turn their knife so that

Example: first-hand experiences

Grating the cheese

this edge was lined up for efficient cutting. The adult was also swift to admire children's competence. One girl was especially thrilled with her success with grating a pile of cheese. Another cried out "Look, look!" as she managed to cut slices of cucumber. Children persevered with folding foil around their sandwich, not an easy task for little fingers. Again the practitioner was on hand to help. One child was swift to give up with, "I can't". In a friendly tone, the adult said, "Yes, you can. There's no such word as 'can't'" and she helped the child to try again – with success.

This activity had been planned in the knowledge that many children were interested in food and food preparation. The nursery team were also aware that some children would benefit from a chance to practise using tools for a good reason. This activity was discussed in the team planning meeting at the end of the afternoon. The practitioner, who led the activity, had noticed that some children could do with more practice in using knives to cut – which need not necessarily be for sandwiches. She also shared that one girl had been sad at the end of the day, because she had not got round to making any sandwiches. The decision

was that, of course, the activity would be offered again very soon.

2. Real gardening

In Ladybirds Pre-School quite a few children were busy during the day, at a time of their choosing, in planting this year's crop of vegetables. The pre-school shares premises with a primary school and the plan was to repeat last year's success with the cooperative school cook. The school kitchen staff do not provide lunches for the pre-school but were happy to cook up the Ladybirds' vegetable crop the previous year. The children were then able to eat their vegetables freshly cooked.

The practitioner had packets with a range of five vegetables and suitable compost in a tuff spot. She explained the steps in the process to the children. This was a good example of a first-hand experience, that is real not pretend, and in which children need to understand the what and why, if the activity is to have a successful outcome: in this case seeds that grow into vegetables that can be eaten. The practitioner explained that they were trying a new method this year which involved each child having a toilet roll cardboard tube, fixing newspaper on the bottom with an elastic band and then putting in compost and their chosen seeds. Over the day individual children chose to do their own planting tubes. The practitioner was ready to demonstrate and explain each time 'new' gardeners arrived. The process sometimes needed the reminder of, "What do we need to do first?" and "What did I do next?", sometimes followed by, "What did I do to stop the newspaper falling off?" (put the elastic band around) and "What do you need to do now you've put your bean in?" (cover it up with compost).

The final step was to write down a label for each planting tube. Some children chose to have a go at writing the label for the vegetable they had chosen to plant. The next step in the process was planned for the following day when the children would dig and place each tube securely into their vegetable garden.

In your team have you explored first-hand experiences for children? Are adult-initiated activities as close as possible to real life, like the examples here? Are practitioners doing too much preparation or expecting children to wait and watch, when they could be fully involved?

practitioners should plan adult-led group times, which children are obligated to join, in order to deliver specific outcomes from particular areas of development. This concern is expressed in some of the early years chatrooms, with the anxiety about "How many group times are we supposed to do?" and "What happens if the children won't join in and cooperate?"

The settings described in this book all had some come-together small group times. But these were intimate key group times for the under threes (Lindon, 2010c). Practitioners responsible for the over threes had planned some group times, but had discussed when these were best timed in the day or week and what was a suitable content. Some examples of group times that work for young children feature on the pages to follow.

Making topic-based planning work

Planning through topics or themes has a relatively long history within early years – long enough that some practitioners equate 'planning' with an approach of planning through specific topics or themes. Planning through topics has never been compulsory for early years practice, although it has become a very familiar format for much of the workforce. In recent times, reflective practitioners and teams have revisited the whole idea of, "Do we actually need topics?", but a topic approach has certainly not been 'banned'.

Some, not all, of the settings described in this book used a very flexible approach to topics as part of their medium-term planning for the over threes, never the younger children. In each case the senior team had developed an approach in which practitioners thought carefully about how a topic would support and extend the learning of young children whom they already knew well.

Practitioners who use topics, or wonder if they should organise in this way, need to think carefully about this aspect to planning. Topics or themes - like any adult-initiated enterprise for young children - have to be judged against two broad questions:

- Is this a good time for these children to explore this area of knowledge and experience?

- Is an adult-planned topic, even a flexible one, a good way for these children to explore this area of knowledge?

Example: group times that work for young children

Big Story Time

1. Big Story Time in Grove House Nursery Class

This now regular end-of-week event first arose from the direct request of children who have now left the centre. About five years ago the team undertook a full consultation with children about their views and feelings. Many of the changes in how the outdoor space is now organised date back to the practical suggestions and preferences of those children. This group also put forward the suggestion that the adults should act out some of children's favourite stories. The special event of Big Story Time evolved and has continued to be a success.

On a Friday, towards the end of each session, all the three-to five-year-olds gather in one large group with some of the practitioners. There is no other time when they are together sitting down in one large group. A couple of practitioners from the Infant and Toddler Centre attend with those key children who will soon join the Nursery Class.

One practitioner holds up a Big Book version of a story that has become familiar to all the children. Week by week they become familiar with the core books that are part of the

medium-term planning. The practitioners read the book one page at a time. Other team members, sometimes plus co-opted staff from other services at the centre, dress up and use props to act out the story page by page.

The book on the day of my visit was *Dear Zoo*, a story of how the zoo kept sending the wrong animals – 'too big', 'too tall', 'too fierce'. So this Friday the dressing up by the adults involved animal face masks, and material to create simple costumes. Each arrival was greeted with enthusiasm by the children as the adult acted out the 'wrong' animal in this scene from the story.

2. Learn-It times in Sun Hill Reception Class

In Sun Hill Reception Class the children have significant choice over their play during the day. They come together in the small key groups at the end of the morning and afternoon. These are adult-guided but relaxed times in which I observed children speaking up with enthusiasm. The phrase Learn-It for the group time came from the children. They had taken it from the regular question of "What did you learn from it", which adults ask individual children who describe their

Example: group times that work for young children

Helpful adults look and listen

specific experiences of the morning or afternoon. Children take their opportunity in these conversational group times to describe what they were doing in the previous half day and what, in their opinion, they have learned.

I listened to one boy describing his chosen focus on drawing a whole series of wiggly lines. He judged he had learned how 'concentrating and looking' were really important. Some children volunteered examples in which they judged that they had learned more about listening or turn taking. So, in children's words and phrases, some of their learning was about social behaviour. Children's views of what they have learned, or want to explore further, are noted on post-it notes by the adult and children place them on their board.

I sat in these group times and observed how practitioners are ready to encourage quieter children by offering their observation of what they noticed a child doing earlier. The adult also helps children to reflect a bit more on what they recall. One adult reminded everyone that sometimes what is important is that you learn something new, but it is just as valuable when you realise you need to practise. Some children

were very articulate about what they had done and learned. Others welcomed open-ended questions from the adult such as, "How did you find out?" and "Have a little think, because you're nearly there." (See also the example on page 18.)

This habit of reflection – five-year-old style – runs through the day. I observed two boys who chose to take one of the carry boxes containing magnifying glasses and colour palettes. The Sun Hill learning environment was planned with the clear view that children needed materials that could travel with them around the indoor and outdoor spaces. The boys chose to go into one of the garden areas and unpacked their box. They used the glasses and colour palettes, exploring the natural environment and then sat together on the covered seat. They asked each other, "What have we learned?" and "What else have we learned?" and discussed their views. A practitioner was in this outdoor space, as well as myself as an observant visitor. But these two boys chose to talk together in this way without the direct involvement of either adult present in the garden.

Within the day individual children had an opportunity to sit with their key person for a conversation about their individual

Example: group times that work for young children

learning plan. Children were able to discuss what they wanted to do, in effect their own short-term forward plan, and the adult helped or advised if that was appropriate. The learning plan is shared with the family, so that they have an input, as do parents when a new topic is started (page 66).

3. Key group time in Garfield Reception Class

The two reception classes within Garfield come together as separate groups at the beginning and end of each morning and afternoon. It is striking that young children - still no more than five years old – enjoy these group times. The content is focussed on their interests and they otherwise have significant amounts of time for free flow play and conversation both indoors and outdoors.

The main content of these come-together sessions was twofold. One part was a focus on planning ahead with individuals who were the focus children this week. It was noticeable that all the children were attentive and contributed to discussions about the enterprises of the focus children. The other focus of some lively discussions was reflecting back with individual children, or small groups of friends, about what they had done during that particular morning or the afternoon.

It is important to note that the practitioners also made their own contribution in an equal partnership with the children. At the beginning of the morning of my visit, the teacher of one class showed the children a wasp's nest and explained how he had found it. The small nest was inside a bug holder and so was easy and safe to pass around the group. Lively discussion followed about the nest and wasps in general.

At the end of the day's come together time for this class, two boys had the opportunity to tell their created stories to the group. Their peers all sat peaceably, listened and occasionally contributed.

- One boy, Michael, chose to sit on the wide chair next to the adult. Michael had a drawing relating to his story, but had not yet worked on a written version. The practitioner affirmed that he would help Michael with a written account and the story could be acted out in full tomorrow.

- The second boy (James) was equipped with his own notes. He stood in the middle of the circle of sitting children and proceeded to explain his characters and choose the actors. The lively story involved Spiderman and Sandman, and James was confident in directing the action. The rest of the group was very involved. The actors – still young children in reception - needed only one friendly reminder from the adult that this was James' story and they should follow his directions for what their characters did in the plot.

4. Questions worth asking

In Oakfield Nursery School, I spent time with a group of eight children, all four-year-olds, who were enjoying a big story book about an owl. Each page only showed part of the bird, along with the habitat and some other creatures. So the children's time with this book encouraged them to make informed guesses.

The children were able to sit in comfort: some were on the carpeted floor, one on a chair and three on a small sofa. The size of the group, and the pace of the story led by the adult, was suitable for children to have the scope and time to comment. The children had come inside from a considerable time playing outdoors and were happy to sit for a while, with this interesting story. The group and seating layout enabled all the children to see the big book. It was easy if they wished, as one or two did, to get up and point to the detail on the current page that had caught their attention and provoked their question or comment.

One child wondered, "Why do mice have tails?" and the practitioner led a short exploration around maybe it helped them to balance when they were running along. A little further along in the story, children wanted to know, "Why do owls have wings?" and "Why do owls fly?" - in contrast with other creatures in the book who clearly ran on feet. A conversation evolved around maybe flying was the way that an owl moved. Another child focussed on the bird's feet, with the talons, pointing out that maybe owls used their feet mainly for carrying things. Another child wanted to know what the owl was carrying in this picture, and several children identified it correctly as a mouse.

- This practitioner welcomed the children's questions and gave time for them to speculate. How do you think this activity would have evolved if she had, in contrast, insisted on being the one to ask all the questions about the story?

Leading a thoughtful approach

POINT FOR REFLECTION

Can children make links of meaning?

Young children – older ones too – are far more likely to extend their current learning when they are able to be active – physically as well as intellectually. Their learning is more secure when they are able to connect the potential of this current experience with what they gained from previous experiences.

There is a very great deal about the world that young children do not yet understand. They need to make connections of meaning between less familiar experiences and their existing knowledge. When children are personally involved in the details and development of their current activity, they are far more likely to make sense of less obvious aspects. An important way for young children to be able to make connections is to have the chance and time to make their own comments and ask their own questions (see the example on page 15).

LINKS WITH YOUR PRACTICE

When practitioners have been trained to use topic-based planning, they sometimes feel the need to convert a child's current consuming interest into a theme that is recognisable to adults. It is important to resist this temptation, because there is a high risk that practitioners will undermine the desire to learn that they believe a topic will support.

For instance, four-year-old Tasha may be keen to explore her current understanding of what happens if you are taken to see a dentist. But she is very unlikely to benefit from having her chosen conversation or pretend play seized and directed into a theme of People Who Help Us – very much an adult big picture of society. Why would Tasha want to go in this direction? She is interested in stretching out from her direct experience of what her dentist did and said; that is Tasha's big picture for the time being.

When you know young children, they will tell you through conversation how they most want to extend an interesting experience. Tasha's key person, or childminder, may realise that Tasha would like to make a personal record about her visit to the dentist. But this next step is not an inevitable one. Perhaps Tasha's comments show that she wants to know more about teeth and is keen to get a book out of the library.

Alert observation and being a genuine conversational partner will give you an insight into what this child understands, what puzzles her and what she wants to know. You follow this thirst for knowledge and it is very possible that some other children will be equally interested in talking about their visit to the dentist or expressing curiosity because they have never been taken.

Timing has to work for the children; the question is not at all about convenient timing for the adults. The topic approach as a whole does not pass the 'good time' question when you spend your days with very young children – the under threes. Babies, toddlers and twos do not have the breadth of general knowledge to make any sense of topics. The associated hopes for learning, even if kept flexible, do not connect with an informed understanding of child development.

For instance, very young children do not do Transport. If they are interested in any kind of vehicle, they may create their own large cardboard box pretend cars. They happily engage with big truck spotting and noisy police car listening when you are out with them on local walks. As their childminder, or key person in a group setting, you embrace the child's interests and ensure a generous supply of large boxes, as well as watching out for any interests around the toy cars and the roadway. This pattern of following children's interests and enthusiasms applies just as much with the over threes.

Topics, or a thematic approach, do not suddenly become the way forward once children have passed their third birthday. Is your proposed topic likely to connect with these children's current level of understanding, will it make sense to them? The answer to "Is

this a good time?" can never just be, "Stories is next on our rolling programme". It needs to be that this group of children, or enough of them, are enthused by story books and that their pretend play shows early signs of the children's ability to create their own storylines. An alternative may be that this group of children have missed out so far on the enchanting world of stories and story telling. In this situation you need to think carefully about how to

Example: enthusiasm for dinosaurs

Constructing the dinosaur cave

Several children in Grove House Nursery Class were very interested in dinosaurs. One child had found a length of green fabric and engaged an adult in making a special dinosaur den. Other children had become interested and were then involved in this play. The team discussed possibilities around dens.

Dinosaurs had been a feature of other patterns of spontaneous play within the week. Some children had constructed a dinosaur cave in the shallow tray on one table indoors. However, this construction had partially collapsed. The decision was made to make resources available so that another cave could be made, and to see where that interest led.

Dinosaurs had also featured in another area. Several children had enjoyed acting out Goldilocks and The Three Bears in the draped comfortable area indoors. An adult had read the story and children played out the scenes. Two of the actors had dinosaurs, which, placed on their heads, became part of this version of Goldilocks.

The nursery class team discussed possible enhancements to the permanent play provision that were likely to support the children's sustained interest in dinosaurs. In each case the short-term planning was closely connected with the particular interest expressed by the children. There was no plan to set in motion a topic about dinosaurs and I agree with the team's approach.

Is your team in the process of rethinking a mainly topic-led approach to planning? When practitioners are most at ease with a topic structure, it can be tempting to plan extensions to children's existing interests in directions that make sense to adults.

- Have you experienced times when extensions in terms of adult-led activities have not been met with much enthusiasm by the children? What did you learn from such times?

- In contrast, what kind of adult-initiated extensions were greeted positively by the children?

- In what ways did these successful ideas connect directly with the details of what children had showed you most intrigued them?

LINKS WITH YOUR PRACTICE

Practitioners need to reflect on how a new experience, introduced by the adults, will connect with what already makes sense to young children. How will this event or activity link to children's existing knowledge and experience of their own world? For instance, under fives do not benefit from celebrating a long list of festivals or special events. One celebration tends to merge into another and unreflective practitioners sometimes have unrealistic expectations about what very young children will learn from the experience (Lindon, 2006).

To be fair, some topic resources set impossibly high aspirations for what under fives will understand about 'other cultures and faiths'. The grown-ups are often rather hazy about the meaning of a secular celebration, let alone complex religious beliefs. The best way is to look for direct connections for children from their personal and family life.

For example, the team in Kennet Day Nursery had celebrated St Patrick's Day because this event had meaning for the setting. Several children and one team member have family roots in Ireland. So it was possible to talk about special days, food, and symbols such as flags in a context of familiar people, and their family life, as well as the reality that some of their relatives did not live locally to the nursery.

Parents have much to share about their children

introduce this adult-led set of experiences, which will be important for children's development in language, foundations to early literacy and sparking the imaginative flow.

Reflective teams, who weave a flexible topic into their overall approach to planning, do not simply import someone else's plan. Any topic has to connect with your knowledge of individual children in your care. If you struggle to think of anything in the children's familiar experience that will connect with 'Under the Sea', then what makes you suppose that these children will be engaged? Perhaps they may be very interested, but you need to start by asking.

Invite children to say and show the sense they make of the possibility that, 'We could find out more about what it's like under the water in the sea.'

- What do they say to you? Let them move around and have the chance to bring you play resources or books, which illustrate what they know or would interest them.

- Spread out what they have brought and see what it tells you about children's experiences to date – what is familiar and what is currently outside their understanding?

- An important question is have any of the children been to the seaside?

- Maybe you need to adjust what looks like a promising magazine feature towards exploration of the seaside itself, before you see if children are interested in what is under the water.

Responsible use of a topic approach is also very careful about creativity and the prospect of any end products.

- Young children need time, space and suitable resources to explore their own creative endeavours. Genuine creativity depends on plenty of scope for young children to decide how to use available materials and to decide what, if anything, will emerge as an end product, as far as they are concerned.

- Young children benefit from open-ended experiences that show them some of the many different forms of art and craft, with adult help for technique as appropriate.

- Some resource books can be supportive for practitioners whose own experience does not include a broad range of crafts. Some crafts cannot be simplified enough for little hands, but many can.

I have observed some very thoughtful, adult-initiated experiences for young children that revolve around art, sometimes resting on the style of a particular artist. These open-ended experiences have been very far removed from a production line of identical Van Gogh sunflowers or from trudging through an inappropriate topic on famous artists. Yes, I did come across that planned theme for under fours and imposed on the baby room too – but not in any of the settings mentioned in this book.

I have been in nurseries where generous supplies of natural materials, and some encouragement by an adult have been all that was needed to enthuse young children to explore the possibilities of outdoor art and sculpture. Thoughtful practitioners have shown children that grown up artists, like Andy Goldsworthy, absolutely believe it is worth their time to create something beautiful from natural materials. Some of these creations do not last long in reality; their longer life is possible through photos. (More about Andy Goldsworthy www.morning-earth.org/artistnaturalists/an_goldsworthy.html).

During my visit to Randolph Beresford, I saw a wall display showing how, within the recent past, the three- and four-year-olds had been introduced to the work of two real artists. The choice was made to show children the work of Mark Rothko and Georgia O'Keefe, because they are both painters who connect colours within a painting in unusual ways and tend to cover the entire canvas. These general features were present in paintings that quite a few children had been making previously out of choice. This adult-led experience offered an introduction for the children to paintings done by Rothko and O'Keefe and the display documented children's interest and their own chosen creations.

The second question, "Is a topic the best way?" needs some thought. My challenge is that some favourite topics are not appropriate ways to plan for young children's learning, once you think properly about the concepts involved. It is usual to see topics on abstract concepts, notably colour and shape. These broad terms apply to some interesting aspects of the natural and created world. But this aspect of children's understanding is far better supported by alert practitioners who 'tuck in' activities behind what currently interests this child or small group.

In an interesting learning environment young children will steadily grasp a wide range of abstract concepts through direct, first-hand experiences. The breadth of concepts they encounter over early childhood is considerably wider than colours and shapes. Children become interested and learn about: height and weight, time and the passing of time, and the evidence of all their senses. Children also have some contrasting experiences around relatively bright or dark, volume of sound, texture, different smells and tastes, and the difficulty sometimes in describing such experiences in words.

The world is full of so many interesting experiences for children. There is no advantage, and considerable drawbacks for young learning, of driving potential interest through packaging up the natural world

- If young girls or boys are currently attuned to colour, you do not need to run a topic on colour. Young children will be busy looking at colour all around them, including the muted shades of the natural world.

- They may choose to organise collections of materials by colour and tone. They may become immersed in active exploration by mixing up paints and blending crayon or chalk colours. You will ensure an extension of basic resources that is attuned to the interests of this child or band of painters.

- Alert practitioners will answer children's questions and make appropriate, timely comments. Your input never needs to include the pointless query of, "What colour is that?" If children are aware of colour names, this knowledge will emerge through their conversation. If they do not yet know, then your abstract question will interrupt and puzzle them.

- If children show no current interest in colour and shade, they may very well be fascinated by something else. There is no sound developmental reason for adults to act as if the most important concepts in a child's world are colour and shape.

- Perhaps this small group of children are currently keen to extend their working knowledge of the properties of water. Today they have chosen to research how many stones it takes to sink a series of toy boats. They certainly do not want to be sidetracked by questions about colour of the week, nor by adults messing with their water by turning it red.

The abstract concept of opposites sometimes appears as a topic and again there is no wise developmental basis for this proposal. Once again, young children learn about genuine opposites through first-hand experience, such as the stark difference between light and dark when day turns into night, or the early dark evenings of wintertime. But they also experience

Example: the Italian restaurant

Food is a personal experience

The team in Oakfield Nursery School support the learning of the over-threes with a flexible approach to a topic that lasts two months each time. Topics do not feature in the planning for the under-threes. Any topic considered by the team always rests on their knowledge of the individual children: there will be good reasons to predict this group will be interested. The team have ideas of what might be new experiences for children and how their learning could be extended. However, these draft ideas are far from final until the broad idea has been shared with the children in open discussion in circle time.

The first step is always to explore with children what they already know about the topic. So the exploration around food with the four- and five-year-olds had started with conversations about what children knew about food, and their current knowledge about the origin of familiar or favourite foods. My visit was towards the beginning of the second month of food as a topic. By then, children had worked with practitioners to create a large wall display where they had drawn and tracked how eggs came from chickens, milk from cows and so on.

They had created an Italian restaurant in one corner, complete with decoration and menus. This focus had come from the children; in an early discussion practitioners heard from them that a pizza restaurant was the most regular place for many children to eat out with their family. So the group agreement was that it would be very interesting to find out more about Italian food.

Once the details of any topic are finalised in consultation with the children, then practitioners write the letter that goes home to families. There is information about what will happen over the two months for this topic, including any decisions that have been made with the children about a role play area.

The letter describes what the team hope that children will learn over this period of time. They also include suggestions for what parents could do, if they wish, within family life. Children do a lot of cooking and baking in Oakfield as part of their normal range of experiences. One of the aims for the food topic was that 'We will learn how to use a blender/food mixer with adult support.'

Example: family involvement over children's interests

Any adult-initiated topic or even very flexible projects need to have direct input from the children, and their families. In Sun Hill Reception Class each half term topic starts with an A4 sheet and letter home to the family. There is a brief explanation about the topic, but the main point is to ask parents to have an informal conversation with their child and write down the question that their son or daughter would most like to investigate.

These sheets are fixed to the display wall headed up with 'so far we have learned'. The personal sheets included writing by parents, emergent writing by the children and drawings to supplement this child's interest. When I visited, the broad topic was transport but the details had been decided by children's chosen line of research. Some examples included, "How many different kinds of boat are there?", "How do underwater trains work, like the one that goes to France", and "How do you ride a bike without stabilisers?" I spent two days in Sun Hill towards the end of term, by which time a considerable number of these searching questions had been answered and documented.

The Sun Hill approach was the wise perspective that a good topic, with depth and interest, would flow through the term.

Over my visit a proportion of the group were very active in running their airport – a focus which had emerged from their expressed interests – organising passport control and the creation of passports for travellers. I observed several children helping their peers with the process of making their passport. At one point, Grace was sat at the passport stamping desk and was very patient in explaining, more than once, to another girl, what needed to fill the passport's blank pages and where the different information should go.

A microphone and simple tannoy system was used by several children for announcements of different kinds. But one run of announcements related to the importance of getting your personal details correct on the passport. One announcer was concerned about how to describe the colour of your hair accurately.

On the second day of my visit, an adult-initiated experience added something extra for children when an old-fashioned motor coach came with the two drivers and was available for small groups of children to explore over the day. Children had a stream of questions for the driver-owners of the coach and they answered them all. The children had time to get on the coach, sit in different parts and directly experience this type of transport.

---

that many apparent opposites are more accurately a continuum. There are many interesting graduations to explore, for instance between completely dry and soaking wet, or really sweet to screw-your-mouth-up sour. Many intriguing mathematical concepts are much more than either/or opposites such as big or small. With a generous store of open-ended materials, children are intrigued to organise and line up the stones and leaves, or the cars, or the little play people and animals.

Wise use of written resources for practitioners

A considerable number of books and magazine articles offer ideas about possible activities to plan with and for young children. Even the most experienced of early years practitioners benefit from some fresh ideas and different angles on familiar experiences. Thoughtful practitioners consider possible resources and make them their own – whether this is part of a topic-based approach to planning or a more general source of potentially good ideas for what to offer to children. Here are some suggested 'do's and 'please don't's. Use them to provoke your own thinking or for discussion within a staff or network meeting.

- Do keep alert to interesting suggestions, whether from a book, a magazine article, or from the internet. Good early years practitioners have plenty of ideas up their sleeve, but they adjust the details for the children they know.

- Don't ever follow someone else's topic resource, or suggested possibilities linked with a story book, as if it is a set of orders that nobody, least of all the children, can disobey.

- Do make the most of our variable weather and the fact that the UK has distinct seasons. Get out in it, go spotting the first spring flowers, make an enormous collection of clean, dry autumn leaves and let the children enjoy them. The rhythms of the natural world are intriguing and provide young children with a direct experience of the timing of growth, and knowledge that you cannot rush events like growing vegetables.

- Don't make this fascinating aspect of real life knowledge and understanding of the world into a fixed topic of autumn or spring that is run in the same way each year. And don't insist that the only way to use the leaves is within a leaf-printing activity, run as a non-creative conveyer belt production line.

- Do reflect on ideas, perhaps from a magazine feature, about introducing vocabulary or open-ended questions around an experience you have good reason to predict will interest the children with whom you spend your days. Use this kind

POINT FOR REFLECTION

Uncertainty can be positive

If early years practitioners are to be genuinely supportive of young learning, they have to be able to live with uncertainty. This adult outlook is crucial for any experiences that claim to support creative development.

An adult-initiated activity fails to support young creativity when young children are instructed how to represent a nursery rhyme – for instance, if the only option is to use the adult's pre-cut template for *Incy Wincey Spider*. Over threes often chose to re-create characters and events they enjoy. It is very possible that they do not want to make a hairy wolf from *The Three Little Pigs*. Perhaps they want to be Mr Wolf and maybe change the story as they play.

Look very closely at any suggestions for adult-led activities linked with a topic where the directions eliminate any uncertainty about what young children will do with the materials. Young children appreciate a generous supply of recycled materials, the means to fix items together and decorate if they wish. Attentive adults can pick up on the interest of, "We want our own rocket" and wonder with the children, "What do you need to make a rocket?" Support for this enterprise is different from firm plans to make a rocket with the children today because that is the next activity in the topic on Space.

of resource as a way to increase the confidence of less sure colleagues. Think about comments you might add to the experience and be very alert to extending children's vocabulary through genuine conversation.

- Don't push in words without a meaningful context. Don't work through a series of suggested questions in a checklist fashion, rather than paying attention to what actual children whom you know are doing in front of you right now.

- Do be pleased when children get enthused and be ready to change your plans and timing in line with what has engaged their interest. Share the control with children – whose play is it anyway? Deal with your anxiety (or again that of a less sure colleague) that responding to children's wishes boils down to losing control.

- Don't carry on regardless with the list of activities and timing that is set out in the written planning or the topic book. Don't behave as if learning is only worthy of respect if adults have planned and predicted this outcome.

- Do keep topic planning in perspective. Even with a good topic idea, everything does not have to be run through this theme. Practitioners get themselves in a serious pickle when otherwise promising adult-initiated activities get twisted to make them fit the current topic.

- Don't act as if enthusiastic child-initiated experiences need the stamp of a topic to become truly valuable. This small group of children are fascinated by spiders. They are highly motivated to go spider and web hunting. However, they want to be spider experts: specialists rather than minibeast generalists.

- Do make a note of what worked well this time around from a resource book or magazine article, without assuming this is now the pattern that will always work. Keep notes of the places where you and the children had a warm welcome, and which people understood how to talk and listen to young children.

- Don't keep running a programme of topics with associated activities, with no thought for possible changes. Deal with awkward feelings in the team if somebody put in a lot of work to get the resource organised a few years ago.

- Do ensure that any bought resource of ideas is brought alive by first-hand experiences that make sense to the children you know. Adjust any details to fit their local neighbourhood. What can you all actually do, what can you visit, what can children directly experience?

- Don't buy or use any resource that claims to have done all the work for you, right down to worksheets that are to be photocopied as 'evidence' of learning. A worksheet that gets children to colour in ice cream cones is good for nothing but paper recycling. Find a simple recipe and make ice cream with the children – that experience is worth everyone's time and energy.

- Do go to an actual greengrocer's shop, or the fruit and vegetable section of a supermarket. Look at the wares, smell them, choose them and bring them back to your home or nursery. Cook or prepare the food, enjoy it.

- Don't set up a greengrocer's role play when you have no reason to suppose that children have ever been to this kind of shop. Certainly don't get them joining up pairs of identical fruit on photocopied sheets.

- Do pay close attention to what the children whom you know appear to be gaining from an adult-led/initiated activity that you chose in the expectation that it would connect with

their interests. In any record of the event, write up what actually happened and how children took the activity off in different directions.

- Don't simply print off a sheet from a website that claims to give you fun learning activities, supposedly set up to fit a specific area and aspect of learning for just any children of this age. Nobody can offer personalised activities in this way; you cannot personalise any possible activity without knowing the person or child as an individual.

KEY POINTS IN LEADING PRACTICE

Managers and other senior practitioners set the tone for practice and guide other members of the team. This chapter has emphasised your role in leading excellent practice that will benefit young children.

- Know your national early years framework: what is non-negotiable, but also the considerable scope for you and your team to decide what to do and how.

- Support less sure practitioners to live with the uncertainty that is part of enjoyable play and genuine conversations.

- Reflect with your team on the balance between adult-initiated activities and generous time for children to choose and organise themselves.

- Ensure that your team values the importance of physical development and physically active play – avoid the trap of lots of 'sitting nicely'.

- Think about the nature of first-hand experiences and whether your provision could improve this aspect of good practice.

- Reflect on how you use group times – how many, when and to what purpose. Are existing group times working for the children?

- If you use topic-based planning, consider whether this approach is working as well as possible.

- Help the team to take a constructively critical approach to potentially good ideas from resource books or magazine articles – and to reject developmentally inappropriate materials.

- Excellent practice evolves one step at a time. Teams need to be pleased together about what has been achieved: your efforts to reflect in depth on what you do, as well as the visible changes you have made.

Books and websites

- Barber J, Paul-Smith S (2010) *Early Years Observation and Planning in Practice*. Practical Pre-School Books

- Bilton H (ed) (2005) *Learning Outdoors: Improving the quality of children's play outdoors*. David Fulton

- Community Playthings *The Value of Block Play* (2005), *I Made a Unicorn* (2008), *Children Come First* (2008), and *Enabling Play: Planning environments* (2010). www.communityplaythings.co.uk

- Cousins J (2003) *Listening to Four Rear Olds*. National Children's Bureau

- Department for Children, Schools and Families (2008, second edition) *The Early Years Foundation Stage – Setting the Standards for Learning, Development and Care for children from birth to five*. DCSF. www.teachernet.gov.uk/teachingandlearning/EYFS

- Department for Education Northern Ireland (2010) *Consultation on the Draft Early Years Strategy*. http://www.deni.gov.uk/index/pre-school-education-pg/16-draft-early-years-strategy-consult-pg.htm

- Duckett R, Drummond M J (2010) *Adventuring in Early Childhood Education*. Sightlines Initiative

- Hope S (2007) *A Nurturing Environment for Children Up to Three*. Islington Council

- Jarman E, The *A Place to Talk* series. www.elizabethjarmanltd.co.uk/

- Kate Greenaway Nursery School and Children's Centre (2009) *Core Experiences for the Early Years Foundation Stage*. Distributed by Early Education, also information available on www.coreexperiences.wikia.com

- Learning and Teaching Scotland (2010) *Pre-birth to Three: Positive Outcomes for Scotland's Children and Families*. www.ltscotland.org.uk/earlyyears/prebirthtothree/nationalguidance/index.asp

- Lewisham Early Years Advice and Resource Network (2002) *A Place to Learn: Developing a stimulating environment*. LEARN

- Lindon J (2001) *Understanding Children's Play*. Nelson Thornes

- Lindon J (2006a) *Helping Babies and Toddlers Learn: A Guide to Good Practice with Under Threes*. National Children's Bureau

- Lindon J (2006b) *Care and Caring Matter: Young Children Learning through Care*. Early Education 2006

- Lindon J (2006) *Equality in Early Childhood: Linking theory and practice*. Hodder Arnold

- Lindon J (2008) *What Does it Mean to be Two? (Three, Four, Five)*. Practical Pre-School Books

- Lindon J (2009a) *What Does it Mean to be One?* Practical Pre-School Books

- Lindon J (2009b) *Parents as Partners: Positive relationships in the early years*. Practical Pre-School Books

- Lindon J (2010a) *Understanding Child Development: Linking theory and practice*. Hodder Education

- Lindon J (2010b) *Reflective practice and Early Years Professionalism: Linking theory and practice*. Hodder Education

- Lindon J (2010c) *The Key Person Approach: Positive relationships in the early years*. Practical Pre-School Books

- Lindon, J (2010d) *Child-Initiated Learning: Positive relationships in the early years*. Practical Pre-School Books

- Manning-Morton J, Thorp M (2006) *Key Times: A Framework for Developing High Quality Provision for Children Under Three Years Old*. The Open University

- Marsden L, Woodbridge J (2005) *Looking Closely at Learning and Teaching: A journey of development*. Early Excellence www.earlyexcellence.com

- Moyles J (2006) 'Is everybody ready?' in Featherstone S (ed) *L is for Sheep: Getting ready for phonics*. Featherstone Education Ltd

- North Tyneside Children, Young People and Learning Directorate (2009) *Enabling Environments: Enabling children*. North Tyneside Council

- OFSTED (2010) *Conducting Early Years Inspections*. www.ofsted.gov.uk/Ofsted-home/Forms-and-guidance/Browse-all-by/Other/General/Conducting-early-years-inspections

- Palmer S and Bayley R (2004) *Foundations for Literacy: A balanced approach to language, listening and literacy skills in the early years*. Network Educational Press

- Rich D, Casanova D, Dixon A, Drummond MJ, Durrant A, Myer C (2005) *First Hand Experiences: What matters to children*. Rich Learning Opportunities. www.richlearningopportunities.co.uk

- Rich D, Drummond MJ, Myer C (2008) *Learning: What Matters to Children*. Rich Learning Opportunities

- Siren Films (2009) *Firm Foundations for Early Literacy* (2010); *Toddlers Outdoors; Two Year Olds Outdoors*. www.sirenfilms.co.uk

- The Scottish Government (2008) *Curriculum for Excellence: building the curriculum 3, a framework for learning and teaching*. www.ltscotland.org.uk/curriculumforexcellence/buildingthecurriculum/guidance/btc3/index.asp

- Warden, C (2005) *The Potential of a Puddle*. Mindstretchers www.mindstretchers.co.uk

- Welsh Assembly Government (2008) *Framework for Children's Learning for 3 to 7-year-olds in Wales; Play/Active Learning: Overview for 3 to 7-year-olds*. Available from: http://wales.gov.uk/topics/educationandskills/schoolshome/curriculuminwales/arevisedcurriculumforwales/foundationphase/?lang=en

Acknowledgements

Acknowledgements

My thanks to the managers and teams of places who made me so welcome and agreed to my using examples from my visits:

Garfield Children's Centre which includes the reception class of Garfield Primary School (North London), Grove House Children's Centre (Southall, London), Kennet Day Nursery (Reading), Ladybirds Pre-School (Southampton), Oakfield Nursery School (Altrincham). Randolph Beresford Early Years Centre (West London), Start Point Sholing Early Years Centre (Southampton) and Sun Hill reception class and Infant School (New Alresford, Hampshire).

A big thank you also to the children in these settings, who accepted my presence in such a friendly way and were keen to explain to a visitor. Any children mentioned in examples have been given fictional names.

My warm thanks to local authority early years teams who have shared their approach to planning with particular emphasis on the learning environment – special mention to Lewisham, Islington and North Tyneside. Finally my thanks to the team at Early Excellence, Outlane, Huddersfield whose innovative approach to resources and the learning environment has helped so many practitioners.

Special thanks to Grove House Children's Centre for allowing us to take photographs in their centre.